Brief Encounters

Short Plays for Beginning Theatre Artists

Darren V. Michael

Austin Peay State University

WAVELAND

PRESS, INC.

Long Grove, Illinois

For information about this book, contact:
Waveland Press, Inc.
4180 IL Route 83, Suite 101
Long Grove, IL 60047-9580
(847) 634-0081
info@waveland.com
www.waveland.com

10-digit ISBN 1-4786-4876-7
13-digit ISBN 978-1-4786-4876-5

Printed in the United States of America

7   6   5   4   3   2   1

Contents

Preface . . . . *.vi*

Special Thanks . . . . *vii*

About the Author. . . . . *viii*

1 + 1 = 2   1

Willie Nelson Ain't Dead · · · · · · · · · · · 2

In a Tree · · · · · · · · · · · · · · · · · · 12

A Widow Safe and Secure · · · · · · · · · 20

Steve Guttenberg Blue · · · · · · · · · · · 30

L'Ours · · · · · · · · · · · · · · · · · · · 40

Out of This World   49

Do I Suffer When I Think About It? · · · · · 50

The Romantic Sway of Near-Earth Objects · · 60

Voice Activated · · · · · · · · · · · · · · · 70

Imaginary Conversations with My Daughter · 82

Attraction · · · · · · · · · · · · · · · · · 92

Intimacy   101

Agnes in Summer · · · · · · · · · · · · · 102

Feathers · · · · · · · · · · · · · · · · · 112

Masterpiece · · · · · · · · · · · · · · · 122

Finally the Day Came
When We Had So Little to Say · · · · · · 132

Lyla Builds a Spaceship · · · · · · · · · · 140

Problems 153

Stuffed Animals · · · · · · · · · · · · · 154

Holly and Jesus· · · · · · · · · · · · · 164

Big Head · · · · · · · · · · · · · · · 174

The Trapeze · · · · · · · · · · · · · · 184

Petunia Pulls Her Punch· · · · · · · · · · 194

There Are No Words For This 203

Adventure· · · · · · · · · · · · · · · 204

Ritual · · · · · · · · · · · · · · · · 208

Preface

Not another directing book. Nope. This is not a directing book. This is not an acting book. Or a book to rival any particular theatre text out there. This is not one of those books.

So, what *is* this particular tome you have in hand? Over my many years of teaching theatre, I've read and used so many different texts in the classroom. Each of them has their strengths. Some of them are heavier in theories of directing or acting. Others offer anecdotes and advice on how to tell stories. Some of them focus on the craft of theatre, introducing terms and concepts that may assist budding directors as they manipulate their "ubermarionettes," as old Edward Gordon Craig might say, around the stage space. Some even focus more on practical exercises for a director to shape the stage and focus an audience's attention or for an actor to bring their characters to life. But almost every one of these texts lack something—actual scripts. That's what we do as directors, actors, and theatre artists. We bring scripts to life. From page to the stage. We get these words on their feet.

Every time I've taught a directing course, I find myself wanting texts. Yes, we could find plays separately. Theatre students should read more plays to expand their artistic vocabulary. We should encourage that. But often valuable time is spent finding a play or scene for an exercise or two when better time could be spent doing the exercises. So, what about a book of scripts specifically designed for the student director or actor? The plays would be short enough to be used for a variety of exercises or open-ended enough to be adapted to the teacher's particular class exercise for the day. The plays could even be used as a supplement to some of the above-mentioned types of texts when they ask for practical work. These plays might be highly specific or offer unique challenges for the young director or actor. The scripts should be flawed, not perfect. Having a young director face a script that has to be really worked on is an incredibly important exercise. We should all be so lucky to work on imperfect plays, even bad plays.

I began writing plays ages ago, after many years as a director and actor. Maybe it's because I just love the crafting of theatre. Or maybe it's because I'm one of those left-brain artists who loves the analysis of the artistic journey and the science of storytelling as much as the creative process, always asking why that worked or why that particular choice made the audience laugh or sigh. As I continued to write, I noticed my writing process, especially when writing short works, always began with an exercise, a limitation I would give myself before I began to write. As an artist, I love limits. I've always loved puzzles and magic because they both ask us to get involved mentally. Solve this or guess how I did this. I've always felt that theatre, puzzles, games, and magic all entertain themselves in the same part of our brain.

What you have here are puzzles, exercises for directors and actors. All the scripts but one have only two characters. Only two of the scripts have a running time over ten minutes and those two are under fifteen minutes. All the scripts have simple sets and for the most part may be cast very flexibly with regard to type, gender, identity, ethnicity, etc. Even though there may be an assumptive descriptor in the cast listing, please feel free to ignore this if the story still works for what you want to do with the piece. My work tends toward playful explorations more than anything else, and I hope this lends the scripts to be evocative mental and physical playgrounds for artists.

Before each piece, I've given a short description of the exercise or potential challenges the play may present for the theatre artist. If these "page-to-stage" challenges and questions help, that's wonderful. Otherwise, toss them and have fun! Feel free to use these plays however you like, whether by themselves or as a supplement to your favorite directing or acting text. The plays are meant to be short and easy to stage for the most part. With the exception of one or two of them, the plays have very few technical demands. If there is a technical element, it was probably part of the initial writing exercise.

The following twenty-two scripts are now yours to use however you wish. I have divided the plays into four groups based on tone, structure, or challenge. Using the entire play or only part of it hopefully proves useful for a variety of theatre exercises.

Special Thanks

Theatre is collaborative. It's why I love the art form so much. And nothing to me is more collaborative than my own writing process. None of the short works could have been possible without the support and time of so many people. Here are some of the wonderful humans who've made my work possible over the years:

Allie Michael, Matilda Michael, Scott Holsclaw, Dr. Johnny Wink, Werner Trieschmann, Steve Burch, Nate Eppler, Chris Bosen, Brian Russell, Keri Pagetta, Mike Montgomery, Jon Royal, Rebekah Durham, The Puzzle Theatre Festival, Roxy Regional Theatre, Elizabeth Walsh Baum, Sean Hills, Daryl Phillipy, Lexi Putter, Logan Reed, Maggie Barnes, Brett Ripley, Erin Tuttle, Will Bates, Talon Beeson, Sara Anderson, Jaylan Downes, Gabby Hannum, Jessica Land, Cassie Hamilton, Lauren Lynch, MadLab Theatre, Ted Kitterman, Bree Presson, Allison Martin, Austin Peay State University Department of Theatre and Dance, Tim X. Davis, and Bluegrass Community and Technical College . . . to name a few.

About the Author

Born in southernmost Arkansas, Darren currently resides in Clarksville, Tennessee, with his lovely wife, Allie, their beautiful daughter, Matilda, and their dog, Stella. His work has been produced across the country, from Nashville, Tennessee to New York City. A professor of Acting and Directing at Austin Peay State University, Darren is a member of the Dramatists Guild of America and the Southeastern Theatre Conference, and the former president of the Tennessee Theatre Association. His full-length play *Scarecrows Will Never See a Sunset* is published through Stage Rights in Los Angeles, California. For those interested in viewing more of Darren's work, please visit www.darrenvanmichael.com.

1 + 1 = 2

The following plays are relatively straightforward—two people, a simple conflict, relatively simple technical demands. The plays focus on a singular goal/obstacle between two people—asking for a dance, renting a room, naming an incoming comet—but they ultimately revolve around a first meeting of two strangers in one room. At times, lines are vague, other times highly specific. There is the awkwardness that comes from a first encounter, but there are opportunities to explore, and revelations that shift power and story, sometimes subtly, other times very much "on the line."

✥ Willie Nelson Ain't Dead ✥

Two People: one man, one woman; minimal set: two chairs and something to represent a bar top/table.

Two regulars find themselves alone and seeking companionship one evening at a local honky-tonk. Bart, thick-headed but as gentle as they come, knows that love may be just around the corner. Matilda, scarred and bitter as a rattlesnake, just wants to dance with as little interruption as possible.

Page-to-Stage Challenges:
- Straightforward lines. Hidden intentions. Brutal honesty. Opposites
- Awkward first impressions and Stanislavski's "moment before." Exploring the environment
- Opposite attraction and tension, like rubber bands
- Environment exercises—dealing with property and setting that are not realized
- Relatively few stage directions, lots of freedom for staging and acting choices
- There's dancing. There's sitting. What else can happen?

Questions to Ponder/Answers to Seek:
- How does the environment affect the characters? The music? The setting?
- How do strangers interact?
- With movement only implied by dialogue, what are the potential explorations each character may entertain or resist?
- How does each character's story arc change as the play advances?
- How does the power dynamic change between the characters from beginning to end?
- How does emptiness and desire factor into each character's choices throughout the plot?

Willie Nelson Ain't Dead
a slow dance

Characters:

Bart   Thirties, looks younger than he really is. A lover of all things country. Innocent to the point of cluelessness, but not stupid. His simplicity is his charm. Things tend to bounce off of him.

Matilda   Thirties or forties, looks older than she really is. Dressed tightly and wearing clothes that are almost too young for her. In a constant search, like a shark who's become bored with the menu. Everything seems to stick to her.

Setting   Present day. A honky-tonk.

A few tables and chairs and a row of stools at a bar. A small dance floor under a cheap disco ball. A jukebox plays soft country music. The bartender seems to be on a break. At opening, we see two people at opposite ends of the bar, neither acknowledging each other at first. BART, dressed in cowboy boots, possibly a cowboy hat, button-down, etc., occasionally glances over at MATILDA, a woman dressed as if she was expecting a wider selection of men with whom to share a dance. MATILDA looks down at her drink, glances around the room, catches eyes with BART, then looks back at her drink. She lets out a long sigh.

BART: Quiet evening.

MATILDA: Yeah.

         She sighs.

BART: (*with a long whistle*)   Seems a shame for a dance floor to be empty.

         No response.

BART: Mighty fine music.

         She continues to stare down at her drink.

BART: (*moving over to her slightly*)   Mind if I buy you one?

3

MATILDA: No, I'm good. I don't think the bartender's around anyway.

She sighs again.

BART: Oh. (*beat*)   Is everything OK?

MATILDA: (*very sarcastically*)   Everything's fine. Nearly perfect. Don't I look just perfect?

BART: Oh, no, you look good.

BART thinks this will open up the conversation. Instead, it dies and MATILDA goes back to looking at her drink. She looks around as if waiting for something or someone.

BART: Waiting for someone?

MATILDA: (*under her breath with a chuckle*)   Mr. Right.

He sees an opening.

BART: How about a dance?

MATILDA: Here we go.

BART: What?

MATILDA: Here we go. I knew it wouldn't be long before one of you good ol' boys made a move.

BART looks around the bar noting the lack of patrons, no bartender, just music.

BART: Well, you come to a honky-tonk dressed like that, you're sending a pretty strong message: "Someone, ask me to dance!"

MATILDA: Is that the message you heard?

BART: Yes, it was.

MATILDA: Well, you must have your wires crossed.

BART: What's the matter with you? I was just trying to ask for a dance. You dance, don't you?

MATILDA: (*conceding*)   Yeah, I guess so.

BART: (*offering again*)   Well?

MATILDA: (*a slight smile*)   OK, but only one. I like to keep my
                options open.

                *MATILDA takes his hand. He leads her to the small
                dance floor under the lights of the disco ball.*

BART: This is nice.

MATILDA: (*not letting herself like it too much*)   Yeah, a little.

BART: So . . . what do you do?

MATILDA: Can we not talk? I just want to dance.

BART: Oh . . . OK. Just dance.

                *They sway softly. MATILDA lays her head on his
                shoulder after a moment. BART feels like the ice has
                broken a bit and starts again.*

BART: So you like country music?

MATILDA: I'm in a honky-tonk, aren't I? Please less talking, more
                dancing.

                They dance a little more in silence. Music.

BART: I was just wondering . . .

                MATILDA sighs in disgust that he won't be quiet.

BART: (*stops suddenly*)   Now just a minute—I—

MATILDA: What? WHAT? What is it?

BART: Well, I—don't know. I just thought I'd make some
                conversation. Did I do something? What happened to
                you to make you so ornery? You seem like you just got
                branded or whipped.

MATILDA: Congratulations. Five minutes before we got a cow or
                horse reference.

                She pulls back away from him and confronts him.

BART: I wasn't saying—

MATILDA: Just who do you think—

BART: No.

MATILDA: Just WHO do you think I am?

BART: Nobody.

MATILDA: What?

BART: Nobody. I don't think you're anybody.

MATILDA: Yeah?!

BART: Yeah, nobody. You're nobody! (*pause*)   OK?

MATILDA: OK. As long as we're straight on that.

> *She grabs his hand and pulls him back to her with some force. She presses herself hard into his chest and continues to dance and listen to the music. BART seems a little confused but continues to dance for lack of a better option.*

BART: (*referring to the music*)   I've seen him seven times.

MATILDA: (*sighs again from the interruption*)   Hmm?

BART: Willie Nelson. Five concerts. Once in downtown Nashville at a record store.

MATILDA: That's just six times.

BART: (*a little hesitant in the confession*)   Oh, well . . . he came to me once in a dream. I guess I count that too.

MATILDA: (*laughs innocently*)   You're so weird. Why do I get the weird ones?

BART: No, seriously.

MATILDA: Oh, I believe you. I believe you saw Willie Nelson in a dream. I once dreamed that George Washington gave me a Swedish massage, but I don't count that as a true brush with celebrity.

BART: (*a little offended*)   I don't just count it because he was in my dreams. That's not it. It was a moment. One of those defining moments. Like right now? Tonight.

MATILDA: Oh, yeah. Right now, huh? You think you have a chance with me?

BART: Well, I admit it's a long shot. But it's just the two of us. We haven't had the best first dance, but who knows.

MATILDA: Isn't he dead?

BART: Willie Nelson?

MATILDA: Yeah.

BART: No, he's not dead. Willie's still kicking and going strong. Raisin' hell.

MATILDA: Can't be raisin' too much hell. He's like a hundred, isn't he?

BART: Nah, he's fine. Saw him last year. He was laughing, singing, like the years hadn't touched him.

MATILDA: Now when you say you saw him, you referring to—I mean, did you really see him or did you dream you saw him? Are you smoking something?

BART: No, no, I really saw him. And I don't smoke. Walked into an old record store when I was in Nashville last summer. There he was. Looking through the blues section. Look, I know what it sounds like.

MATILDA: Sounds crazy.

BART: Yeah, yeah, but hear me out. Have you ever felt like you were lost? Like you're in the middle of an intersection but there are roads moving off in every direction like you're in the center of a wheel with hundreds of spokes shooting off in every direction around you? And all you feel like is that you're spinning there. Spinning so fast that you can't focus, completely overwhelmed. You may see people but no faces. Cars but no drivers. And then you think you're moving but all you're doing is drowning. Sinking, spiraling down. So many options, you don't have any options. In that worst moment, at the moment of complete collapse, like you just want to give up on things, that's when I saw him. (*he sings softly, not very well but sincerely*)   Just like a lighthouse you must stand alone. Or something like that. Heck, it could have been "Whiskey River" or "On the Road Again." To be honest, I wasn't in my right mind at the time. Drunk as a skunk. But I felt better after I woke up.

MATILDA: And Willie Nelson did that for you.

BART: Sure. As good an explanation as anything else.

MATILDA: (*conceding*) Yeah, I guess so. (*noticing that the only music playing is Willie Nelson's songs*) Is that all that old juke box plays? Willie Nelson?

BART: No, but that's all it plays when that's all you select. I put ten dollars in it and selected tracks D1 through D20. Willie's greatest hits.

MATILDA: I'm more of a Hank Jr. fan.

BART: I guessed that.

MATILDA: Oh, you did. How?

BART: The way you're dressed. Definitely not a fan of the Red Headed Stranger. Hank tends to attract a different crowd.

MATILDA: A different crowd?

BART: Yeah, like Hooters' waitresses.

MATILDA: (*pretending to be insulted*) Hooters' waitresses?

BART: (*trying to apologize*) No, I didn't mean—

MATILDA: Relax, cowboy. I'm just messing with you. (*after a pause and letting him off the hook*) They have good food. I love their wings. (*she smiles at him*) I worked there after high school.

BART: You did?

MATILDA: What does that mean? "You did?" I could work at Hooters.

BART: No, I didn't mean that you couldn't. Of course, you could. I mean you have the . . . I mean, you seem . . . I mean, the food is great. I love the wings.

MATILDA: The food is great. And thank you.

BART: For what? I don't think this seduction is going very well.

MATILDA: (*laughing*) No, you're doing just fine. Stop trying so hard. And thank you for not thinking I could work at Hooters. I think that was a clumsy attempt at a compliment.

BART: Well, I, I just—Man, this is not my night.

MATILDA: You just keep dancing. The night's not over. And Willie's still playing on the jukebox.

BART: I've seen Jr. four times.

MATILDA: All in this world or did he also visit you in a time of need?

BART: Nah, all in concerts. I don't see Hank as a dream-visiting kind of guy. He's got too much on his plate.

MATILDA: (*laughing*)   So weird.
                (*to no one in particular*)   How do I get stuck with them?

BART: So you were hoping for something else.

MATILDA: Well, yeah. No. I don't know. Just thought I'd show off this new dress.

BART: Well, for your sake, I'm sorry there aren't more to see it. But if truth be told, I'm glad I'm the only one.

MATILDA: What's your favorite Willie song?

BART: That's a hard one. It's Willie. That's like trying to pick your favorite hundred-dollar bill. I guess I'd say "Just Like Over the Mountaintops." Love that song.

MATILDA: That's not the name of that song.

BART: What? Sure it is.

BART hums to himself as reassurance.

MATILDA: That's not the name of that song.

BART: Yes, it is. I'm the biggest Willie fan in the world. That is the name of the song, lady. (*realizing*)   I don't know your name.

MATILDA: Matilda.

BART: Matilda? Isn't that a kangaroo? The "Dancing Matilda"?

MATILDA: No, lunkhead. The song's "Waltzing Matilda." It's Australian. I think it's some sort of reference to a blanket or something. Not very pretty.

BART: Eh, it's OK. It's nice. Different.

MATILDA: Wow, I think I'm going to swoon with delight. Your name?

BART: Bart. Bart the lunkhead cowboy.

MATILDA: (*smiles*)   OK, well, "Over the Mountaintop" is not the name of that song.

BART: It isn't. What is it?

MATILDA: (*playfully*)   I'm not telling you now. Just shut up and dance.

> *He pulls her back to him and they continue to dance.*

BART: You come here often?

MATILDA: (*sighing with the admission*)   All the time. You?

BART: First time.

> *She smiles to herself. After a moment, Matilda begins to sing softly as they dance. BART immediately recognizes the song, sung perfectly.*

MATILDA: It's called "Till I Gain Control Again," Mr. Biggest Willie Fan in the World.

> *They continue to dance as the lights fade.*

BLACKOUT. END OF PLAY.

✑ In a Tree ✑

Two people, minimal set: a ladder, platform, or chair for the "tree."

One is in a tree. The other person wants in it. It's really a question of who came first and who gets to make the rules.

Page-to-Stage Challenges:
- Very few stage directions—lots of staging flexibility.
- Simple dialogue, but a few difficult lines to make honest— foreign language, odd terms, etc.
- A seemingly small goal/obstacle that becomes more and more complex.
- A silly circumstance that means a great deal to the participants.

Questions to Ponder/Answers to Seek:
- What value does each character place on their position in the world?
- How is power used and manipulated throughout the play?
- What tactics does each character use to hold sway over the other?
- How do the different levels prohibit or allow for staging? What are the challenges of this spacing dynamic?
- How does the environment affect the characters?

In a Tree
a negotiation

Characters:

A   A person in a tree. Could be anyone.

B   A passerby. Could be anyone else.

Setting   Some place with a tree. Other trees may be nearby.

PRODUCTION NOTE: Feel free to decide how to stage this, with or without a "tree." All that is important is that A (in the tree) is much higher than B as they pass by.

A is in a tree. B approaches.

A: Who goes there?

B: Wait. What?

A: State your purpose.

B: Out for a walk. (*surveys the situation and then faces a decision*)   May I come up?

A: First! Answer my questions.

B: Or what?

A: I get to throw . . . (*scrambling looking for something in the tree*)   this at you.

> *A holds up some sort of instrument of indeterminate origin, possibly a weapon.*

B: That doesn't seem so bad. What is that?

A: I call it the BOOM 3000. It's rock hard. Bitter cold. Heartless.

B: That seems really extreme.

A: I needed the stakes to be high.

B: So these questions. What kind of questions are we talking here?

A: Serious ones.

B: I mean you're a little too old to be up in a tree and be taken seriously.

A: You want in this tree?

B: Well, I'm not sure now. It's a nice day for a walk. Maybe I'll just keep walking.

A: It's a great tree. Big. Sturdy. Great view. You can feel the breeze up here.

B: That does sound nice.

A: It's pretty fantastic if you ask me. Better than a walk.

B: Wow. OK then. You've sold me.

A: So you want the questions?

B: Sure.

A raises BOOM 3000 as if to hurl it at B.

B: (*continued*)   WHOA! I haven't answered a question yet.

A: You'll get them wrong.

B: I'm pretty smart.

A: Maybe they're trick questions. No real answers. Maybe I just want to test my newly developed BOOM 3000 against you, protect what I have.

B: You don't seem like the sort to do that. I mean you climb a tree and wait for someone to pass. You even developed this "test" of questions. Sounds like you have a lot of time on your hands in that tree. Sounds like you're lonely.

A: That's a risky hypothesis. You haven't even heard the questions yet.

B: That's fair. So . . .

A: You answer the questions correctly—

B: And I can climb your tree. Got it.

A: That's not all.

B: There's more?

A: Maybe. You'll have to find out. After you answer the questions.

B: There seems to be an awful lot of prescreening just to get into this tree.

A: It's a pretty darn great tree.

B: Well, now I can't leave. I have to get in that tree. What's stopping me from refusing to answer your questions and just climbing up there with you?

A: My newly developed BOOM—

B: Oh, yeah, right. These questions. Are they trick questions?

A: No. In fact, they are relatively simple. Just three.

B: Let's do this.

A: Ready?

B: Fire away. Questions. Not the . . . BOOM 3000.

A: OK. First question.

B is so excited for this.

A: (*pig Latin*) O-day ou-yay ike-lay o-tay ing-say in-yay e-thay ower-shay?

B: Wait. What?

A begins to raise the BOOM 3000.

B: (*continued*)   No, no. I didn't know the questions weren't in English. Is that pig Latin?

A is silently defiant.

B: (*continued*)   OK, OK. I got this. Can I ask you to repeat it?

A: (*conceding but not happy about it*)   O-day ou-yay ike-lay o-tay ing-say in-yay e-thay ower-shay?

B: (*piecing it together*)   Do you . . . I . . . do I like . . . to . . . sing . . . in the . . . shower? Do I like to sing in the shower? Um . . . yes. I think I do. I answer yes. Next question.

A: (*with fluency*)   Quelle est votre couleur préférée?

B: What?! Is that French? That's not fair.

A begins to raise their arm to throw BOOM again.

B: No, wait. Fine. I can figure this out. Again please.

A: Quelle est votre couleur préférée?

B: Couleur? Couleur. Color! Color. Préférée. Préférée. Prefer. Prefer. Color prefer. Prefer color. Favorite color! PURPLE! I love purple! One more question and I'm climbing that tree.

A smirks and shakes their head in defiance.

B: Come on. I got this. Let's go. Last one.

A: (*sighs, then with ease once again*)   Kwanini unataka kupanda mti huu?

B: You're just making up words now.

A shakes their head.

B: (*continued*)   That's a real language?

A nods.

B: I don't trust you.

A shrugs their shoulders.

B: There has to be some sort of trust involved otherwise why am I even going through this. There was an understanding when this started. There was access to a tree. This tree. A few questions might grant me access to this fine tree. Now they're in other languages. This is a pretty big hurdle just to climb a tree. And not get something thrown at me.

A: Give up?

B: These rules seem to be completely arbitrary.

A: Completely. I was in the tree first. My rules.

B: Gosh. I don't think that tree is really worth the effort now that I've begun this whole process. What about that tree over there?

A: Where?

B: Over there. There's a whole grove of them over there. Maybe one of them will be better.

A: No way. This is the best tree.

B: Yeah, but we've really strayed so far from where we began. I think I'll go over to the other tree. You can continue to spend your time up in your tree all alone. Maybe I'll invite people to get in my tree for free. I'll put up signs. Anyone can climb my tree.

A: Well, that's insane. You going to let ANYONE just wander up and start climbing?

B: Yep. Anyone and everyone.

A: What about the weirdos? Or the cool chicks? Or the politicians? What about the infirmed? How are they going to get into your tree?

B: Maybe I'll help them up. I'll climb down and then I'll boost each one up into the tree.

A: They could fall. They can't grab hold very well. They will fall and hurt themselves. They will probably sue you or cry out against your tree. Make you chop it down. They will protest your tree. Cries of "No more trees! Down with the trees!" will echo and keep you awake at night.

B: I guess that's the chance I have to take. It's just a tree.

A: Even the jerks? The A-class donkeys? The flat-earthers? The sideshow freaks? The duck-lipped posers? Social media whores? Even Kanye? You have to draw a line.

B: That does cause me some anxiety. But maybe being in the tree will make them see things differently?

A: But in order to get to your tree they have to go past my tree! I can't have that.

B: I don't think you have much choice. Everyone is welcome in my tree.

A: How about this? I just let you up here. Forget about that last question, it was Swahili, by the way . . .

B: Oh, man! Swahili. Of course. A pause.

A: You join me and forget about that other tree.

B: That's sounds pretty great. And a lot less trouble.

A: Exactly. A lot less. This tree already has a system in place. Yes, it has its kinks and flaws but it's working for the most part. Who knows? Maybe just by you being here could improve how this tree works.

B:	So you're open to change?
A:	Well . . . let's see once you're up here. You get settled in. Look around. Take in the fresh air, the view. Things look so different from up here. We'll see how it goes.
B:	I don't know.
A:	Come on. What have you got to lose?
B:	(*thinking about it briefly*) Nothing, I guess. Huh. It's pretty much a win-win for me.
A:	I love a win-win. Especially one that ends up with me still in this tree.
B:	So I don't have to answer that question. What if that gets around?
A:	What do you mean?
B:	What if others find out that the rules are a little flexible?
A:	Who's going to find out? There's no one here.
B:	And the . . . BOOM 3000?
A:	What about it?
B:	It's not a threat anymore?
A:	Oh, I have to throw it at you . . . at least one time. In order for something to be meaningful you have to suffer a little. To appreciate the reward, you have to sacrifice.
B:	What did you sacrifice?
A:	Nothing. I was here first. I get to decide.
B:	That doesn't seem fair.
A:	I never said anything about fairness. This all began when you walked past this tree. Then I say this, you say that, bada bing. Here we are.
B:	And so my sacrifice is—
A:	Getting hit in the face with my BOOM 3000.
B:	Will it hurt much?
A:	If it didn't hurt would it be a sacrifice? (*that doesn't help B's disposition*) OK, it won't hurt much. It's probably just made out of foam or rubber, right? It's an incredibly small price to pay.
B:	Well, then I think we have ourselves a deal.

A: Excellent.

B: But what happens the next time someone walks by the tree?

A: Same thing. Rinse and repeat.

B: Can I make up the questions? If I'm going to take a BOOM 3000 to the face so I can scale this tree at least let me make up the questions.

A: (*hesitant to relinquish power*)   Fine. You can make up the questions. But I will test the BOOM 3000 on you. That's a deal breaker. There has to be some compromise. Hello, my tree. I have to get something out of this.

B: What if you just, I don't know, throw something else at those wanting in the tree? Something with potentially less dangerous results.

A: This is becoming way more complicated than I wanted. Honestly, I really just wanted to throw this at someone. The tree, the questions I made up while I was waiting for someone to pass by. You got me. I guess I don't get to try out my BOOM 3000.

B: No, go ahead. I still want in the tree. I'm not going to back out now.

A: Really? Even though you know the truth?

B: You seem to have a good thing going. Tell you what—I'll take your place. You won't have to stay in the tree anymore. You can just wander around and throw things at people.

A: That's awesome, dude. Thanks so much.

B: Don't mention it. But you owe me.

A climbs down as B climbs up.

B: Hey, you didn't use the BOOM 3000.

A: You know what? Well, let's say you owe me twice. Enjoy your tree.

A exits. B proudly surveys the landscape atop the tree. Then . . .

B: Not the best view.

BLACKOUT. END OF PLAY.

❧ A Widow Safe and Secure ❧

Two people: one woman, one man; simple interior set: a few chairs for "furniture."

Willow has recently lost her husband. With her soul mate gone, she struggles to find purpose and her former sense of adventure she remembers from years ago. When a Syrian immigrant knocks on her door seeking a room to rent, Willow takes the smallest steps to stand on her own once more.

Page-to-Stage Challenges:
- Older characters
- Potential dialect work
- Listening and deciphering the scene partner
- What's not being said as fuel for the lines
- Motivations and intentions that aren't exactly on the line
- Lots of staging options

Questions to Ponder/Answers to Seek:
- How does the setting empower or weaken each character?
- Are there opportunities for each character to explore the space as both familiar and unfamiliar territory?
- How does each character's internal struggles impact what they do or how they interact with the other character?
- In what ways can pacing and interaction affect the shape of the scene?
- What opportunities are in the script for the characters to fight for personal victories?

A Widow Safe and Secure
a crossroads

Characters:

Willow   Fifties, beautiful but dulled by sadness. A woman with
          an adventurous, almost whimsical spirit shackled just
          the slightest by the recent passing of her husband. A
          woman who has forgotten her best qualities and fallen
          into a despair so deep she is oblivious to its effect.

Khalil   Thirties, attractive Middle Eastern man with a quiet,
          alluring nature. He exudes a peace that is almost unnat-
          ural. Although he is fluent in the English language and
          usually speaks with confidence, like many people who
          are new to actually using a second language, he may not
          completely understand the nuance of the language. He
          seeks to comfort people and only stumbles when he fails
          at that. Otherwise, he speaks with a haunting peace.

Setting   A brownstone apartment in a large city in the early 2010s.

> *The living room of a small brownstone apartment.*
> *WILLOW sits on a sofa talking on a phone to her friend.*

WILLOW: (*sighs*) I don't know what to do now. We did just
          about everything. Now I've got wonderful memories
          and a home that's too big for one person. I can't sell
          it. I don't want to live anywhere else. Maybe renting
          that extra room is a good idea. Howard said we should
          have years ago. A little extra income, someone to keep
          an eye on the place while we're gone. But I always
          liked our life together. The two of us. Facing the world.
          (*sighs again*) What do you do with half your life
          when the one you thought you were going to spend
          it with is gone? (*responds to her friend's question*) Yes,
          I guess so. A new chapter, right. OK. Are you coming
          by this evening? Oh, they are? Of course. Oh, stop it.
          (*putting on a smile*) Oh, stop it. Of course, you go be
          with your boys. I'll figure out something. There are
          still tons of boxes to go through and a lot of stuff that
          needs to be trashed. I've got plenty to do. Go, go. Have

fun. We'll connect tomorrow. Hazel, please. You are not abandoning me. Please, no drama. Really, I have a ton to keep me busy. No, no. You should be with your boys. As appealing as that offer really is, I think I want to stay in tonight.

WILLOW hangs up the phone and sits alone, not stirring for a moment. She turns back to face the empty room. Stares for a minute. Realizing how empty the room is and how little she wants to tackle her current situation, she slowly exits to her bedroom. There is a brief silence, then a knock at the front door.

WILLOW reenters and goes to the door.

WILLOW: Just a minute. I'm coming. Be right there.

WILLOW opens the door to find KHALIL, dressed neatly, with an air of peculiarity.

KHALIL: (*with the slightest accent*)   Hello. My name is Khalil Al-Bayat. I'm here seeking the room.

WILLOW is stunned by the request and the stranger.

KHALIL: (*continued*)   Hello? The room? For rent? Is it still available?

WILLOW: (*finally and a little embarrassed*)   Oh, yes. The room. I, uh . . . I hadn't really been thinking about it. I'd really just forgotten. We haven't had many people asking about it.

KHALIL: Is it still available?

WILLOW: Uh, yes. Yes, it is. (*brief pause*)   I'm sorry. Your name again?

KHALIL: Khalil. Khalil Al-Bayat. Is this a good time? I know it's a little late in the afternoon.

WILLOW: Late? No. Uh, pardon me. I'm a little distracted today.

KHALIL: Distracted. Yes. I had been meaning to come by yesterday, but first day at my new job. Today is finding the place to stay. A little backwards possibly. But here I am. Is the room still available?

WILLOW: Oh, yes. Uh, please. Come in. Have a seat . . . Mr. Bayat.

She opens the door wide for him and shows him to a couch in the middle of the room.

KHALIL: Al-Bayat. The full last name is Al-Bayat. But please call me Khalil.

WILLOW: I'm so sorry, Mr. Al—Khalil. You can call me Willow.

KHALIL: (*notices the boxes*) Willow. A very interesting name. Are you going somewhere?

WILLOW: Oh, no. Just organizing, getting rid of a few things.

KHALIL: Oh, if this is not a good time, I could come back another time. I could go back down to the shelter.

WILLOW: The shelter? You're staying at the shelter?

KHALIL: (*only slightly embarrassed*) Oh, why, yes. I haven't been in the city very long. Didn't really have any place to go. I didn't want to spend my money on a hotel room. Hoping to find an apartment to lease as soon as possible, you see. It's not that bad.

WILLOW: It's terrible. Ah, my goodness. Well, OK . . . let's see what we can do.

WILLOW doesn't know how to proceed from this point.

KHALIL: Madam? Are you OK?

WILLOW: Well, I must admit I'm a little out of my element. What do we do from here? Frankly I hadn't thought about that ad for a few days. It's only been in the papers since last week. Right before . . .

An awkward pause. KHALIL tries to figure out why but instead decides to break the silence.

KHALIL: (*helping her*) Well, introductions maybe? I'm from Damascus. Syria. Born there. I have been in the U.S. for about a week now. I am happy to report I am the newest employee of Bailey Electronics on Forty-Sixth and Sixth Street.

WILLOW: (*awkwardly, but honest*)   Well, welcome to our country, I guess.

KHALIL: Thank you very much. It is a most interesting place you have here.

WILLOW: So you are looking for an apartment? How long?

KHALIL: Excuse me?

WILLOW: How long? Of a lease? Six months? A year?

KHALIL: Oh, I am looking for a home. I think I will be here forever in the U.S. Permanently. This is now my home.

WILLOW: Well . . . splendid. Um, I'm very sorry for being so bad at this. Normally, I'm much more on top of things.

KHALIL: (*politely*)   There is no need to explain. I believe you are doing just fine.

WILLOW: But we will not have you staying in a shelter. How inhospitable would that be? So new to the country, new in the city, and then thrust into a shelter. No, no, no.

KHALIL: (*getting up*)   May I look around?

> *WILLOW nods. KHALIL slowly moves around the room, scanning boxes and surveying the place.*

WILLOW: There are two bedrooms to the place. It was a guest room. I wanted to rent it out before but . . . you know for a little extra income but never really got around to doing it. Mostly because it doesn't have its own bath and you'd have to share a kitchen. It's small but nice. Had it refurbished a few years ago.

KHALIL: (*listening and moving around*)   Mm-hmm. This room here would be mine?

WILLOW: Yes. It is a very nice room. Do you like America?

KHALIL: Hmm?

WILLOW: Do you like it here? So far?

KHALIL: Well, my brief experiences have been the immigration office, a shelter, a small electronics store, and your lovely home and hospitality.

KHALIL smiles and WILLOW seems a little embarrassed but this does seem to make her relax a bit.

WILLOW: What brings you to this country?

KHALIL: Have you watched the news lately? Syria isn't the best place to be right now. I love the place of my birth but it is a difficult time. The Arab Spring has become the Arab Summer and the Arab Fall and so on. If I want to get on with my life I must leave.

WILLOW: Oh, goodness. That's very sad.

KHALIL: A little, yes. But I am an American now. Well, will be one day, I hope.

WILLOW: Aren't you angry? I think I would be angry.

KHALIL: Angry? Why?

WILLOW: At us? At the U.S.? I always hear that we've really screwed things up over there. How everyone hates us.

KHALIL: (*laughing slightly*)   Well, there would be no popularity contest you would win, but I think Americans think they are more important than they really are. The Syrians, the Arab world has more to think about daily than what is America doing. I think that is a distraction.

WILLOW smiles and seems intrigued.

KHALIL: (*continued*)   Only one door?

WILLOW: Yes. No back entrance. But don't worry I'm a heavy sleeper if you're coming and going late hours.

KHALIL: No, no late hours for me. I don't really have the time. (*noticing a picture or something*)   Have you ever been to the Middle East?

WILLOW: No, I haven't. I've been to a lot of places, never there. I find America boring. Lonely even.

KHALIL: Really? I find it stimulating. Frightening but definitely stimulating. (*suddenly as if sensing her struggle*)   You seem ill at ease with my presence. Maybe this was not meant to be as they say. I will keep looking. I thank you for your time.

WILLOW: What? No. Don't go. You haven't seen the bedroom yet, the bath. I'm being terribly odd, I know. (*trying to make things comfortable again*) Any family? Wife? Oh, of course not. She'd be with you. Brothers? Sisters?

KHALIL: Two brothers. I was married.

WILLOW: Ah, me too. Was married. It is a brutal awakening to one day find yourself on your own. Don't you think?

KHALIL: Yes. Brutal.

WILLOW: You find yourself second guessing everything. Before, you would just open the door and head out to whatever was waiting, go wherever the wind took you. Then all of sudden, you're looking over your shoulder. Making sure the next person you come in contact with doesn't want to harm you or kidnap you, violate you in some way.

    KHALIL is unnerved just slightly by her confession.

KHALIL: Yes . . . I guess. (*nervously attempting to make a joke*)   You aren't one of those people, right? Just a generous woman looking for a tenant.

WILLOW: Oh, why, yes. And you aren't one of those people either, right?

KHALIL: (*after a pause for effect*)   No. I think not. At least not until after we talk price.

WILLOW: (*laughing*)   Oh. He-he. Yes. I think you're harmless.

KHALIL: I wouldn't say harmless. I know what you Americans think of an Arabic man. The Homeland Security airport screener was very gentle in his strip search.

    WILLOW is shocked then realizes he's joking with her.

WILLOW: Do you miss your home? Your family? Your wife?

KHALIL: Do you miss your husband?

    Neither has to answer.

WILLOW: Sometimes we find ourselves in a place we didn't want to be.

KHALIL: Sometimes that's exactly where I think we should be.

WILLOW: I used to think that way. Funny thing, thirty years ago I never thought I would marry. Never even entertained having children.

KHALIL: How many do you have?

WILLOW: One. Jessie. He's a good son. But he's busy a lot. Very successful. Always on the go. I think I taught him that.

KHALIL: You are no longer "on the go"?

WILLOW: No. I just um . . . well, I'm not. What brought you to the states? Oh, well, I've already asked that, haven't I?

KHALIL: You do not like being alone now, but you did once?

WILLOW: It isn't that I liked being alone. I liked having no strings, or fewer strings.

KHALIL: Strings. Attachments. Was your husband a string? Your son?

WILLOW: (*insulted*)   What? What are you implying? No, I love my husband, my son. The nerve of you.

KHALIL: I meant nothing. I am trying to listen, uh, understand. I came to look at an apartment. You talk about your family and strings and your loneliness. I apologize. I should not have said what I said. I should have not pried. If I was inappropriate, I'm very sorry. Just a few days here. Things were going well, then this catastrophe.

WILLOW: (*trying to mend the situation*)   No, I'm the one who was inappropriate. I find I like people so much less now. Isn't that awful? And I'm taking it out on you. I was never this bitter, this mean, this frail. It infuriates me. I just need to—

> WILLOW *starts to yell but grits her teeth instead and holds in the explosion.*

KHALIL: I find people quite full of beauty. Unique.

WILLOW: Well, you're either crazy or naive.

KHALIL: (*laughing a bit*)   Possibly. But I still find myself here in your apartment and in need of a room.

WILLOW:	I honestly never thought of renting to a man. Not that I'm against men, but being a single woman, a widow, it just seemed strange.
KHALIL:	I see. Well, I can understand that. I'm a bit of a recluse myself. I will go if it's uncomfortable for you.
WILLOW:	It is. A little. (*a pause*) But stay.
KHALIL:	I will be an ideal tenant. I'm clean. I'm foreign so that has to be good for your security. I may keep strangers at bay. (*she laughs at his attempt at a joke*) I don't watch TV. I can cook.
WILLOW:	Well, I do like TV. I read.
KHALIL:	I read as well. We can share authors.
WILLOW:	Yes. I guess so. OK . . . well, the rent is $1,200. A month.
KHALIL:	(*a bit taken back at the sudden shift*) Oh . . . no. Thank you.
WILLOW:	I think it's a fair price.
KHALIL:	I will give you $600 a month. Final offer.
WILLOW:	$600?! That's ridiculous. You won't find anything around here in that price range. $1,200. Nothing less. (*this haggling has given her a chance to be brave again*) I think you have underestimated me, Mr. Al-Bayat. I may look like I'm easily taken but you'll find I'm a little tougher than most women.
KHALIL:	I can see that. You've been around the world.
WILLOW:	Are you making fun of me? Who do you think you are? I think you should go.
KHALIL:	I am not. No, please. You misunderstand. We haggle, right? Mr. Tarvoli at the store said I should make sure I am not taken advantage of.
WILLOW:	I would never do that. You want a room to rent. You want to get out of the shelter. The room is $1,200 a month.
KHALIL:	But you don't like people. I'm people. I was not sure your intentions.
WILLOW:	My intentions are to rent you this room for $1,200.

KHALIL: I'm not sure I can afford that. I don't get my first check for two weeks. I just have what I have saved. $800 a month?

WILLOW: I thought you liked people. You think they are unique.

KHALIL: Yes, beautiful and unique, but that doesn't mean they won't take advantage of me.

WILLOW: I am not that type of person. I am not a beautiful, unique person. I won't take advantage of you. I just need that room filled.

KHALIL: I—uh—I am not sure what to say. $850?

WILLOW: Eight fifty? You think that's fair.

KHALIL: No, I think that's what I've got to offer.

WILLOW: (*she thinks for a moment*)   I will not be taken advantage of. No. (*a pause*) $900 a month. Take it or leave it.

KHALIL: Yes. Thank you, Mrs., uh, Miss Willow.

WILLOW: Thank you, Mr. Al-Bayat.

KHALIL: (*trying to lighten the mood*)   Your husband would be proud of such a tough negotiator.

> WILLOW *smiles slightly. She starts to exit to a room but then—*

WILLOW: Mr. Al-Bayat? May I ask how your wife died?

KHALIL: (*gently but very matter-of-factly*)   She was murdered on the street outside our home by men who did not appreciate her being without a man to escort her.

WILLOW: People are beautiful?

KHALIL: And unique.

WILLOW: I will get your key.

> WILLOW *exits as* KHALIL *stands alone.*

> *BLACKOUT. END OF PLAY.*

❦ Steve Guttenberg Blue ❧

Two people: one woman, one flexible; simple set.

When a young assistant is sent to a local hardware store on a rather cryptic errand, they realize that a generational gap is a huge obstacle to solving this particular puzzle.

Page-to-Stage Challenges:
- Lots of opportunities for staging. Wide open
- Strangers working together for a common goal
- Potential research on dated cultural references
- Awkward exchanges and confessions
- Vague ending dialogue

Questions to Ponder/Answer to Seek:
- What is the relationship between the two characters professionally and how does this affect the scene? How does it change as the play progresses?
- How do the characters move from strangers to allies in the piece?
- How do the characters grapple with the unknowable?
- How can tempo and pace be adjusted to affect the relationships, the story, and the internal and external struggles in the play?
- What environmental elements may or may not be affecting the characters?

Steve Guttenberg Blue
a mystery

Characters:

Egg   Twenties, female, an office assistant.

Tiff   Twenties, a hardware store employee.

Setting   The paint aisle of a local hardware store.

AT RISE, we see EGG staring at a row of paint swatches. She is very neatly dressed, a suit maybe, what the expectations of her job demand. She seems lost, struggling to decipher a puzzle. She holds several paint swatches in her hand. After a beat or two, TIFF enters. They have the brightly colored vest that denotes their employment at the hardware store. TIFF waffles a bit, doesn't want to be a nuisance but also knows the job. And so . . .

TIFF: I'm here if you need me.

EGG nods but then goes back to the swatches.

TIFF: (*continued*) We have a wide variety of colors, tones, textures, etcetera.

EGG: (*mumbling*) Blue.

TIFF: Blue? Well, as you can see there are so many options. It really depends on the project you have in mind. For example, for a bedroom you may want something a little deeper in tone, but for a blue in a family area I would lean more toward a pastel or a . . .

EGG is not really listening.

EGG: I need to find this blue. I'm painting my boss' office. Well, I'm not actually painting it. But I've been given an "assignment." I'm just looking for this one.

TIFF: Choosing the right one is a very personal decision.

EGG: Yeah, no. Not a personal decision. He insisted on a very specific color. Well, I think it was specific. (*mumbling again*) I have no idea what this means. . . . Blue is blue, right?

31

TIFF   Well as I said . . .

EGG hands TIFF a slip of paper.

EGG: Do you have this? This color? This blue?

TIFF: (*looking at the piece of paper*)   I don't know what this is.

EGG: (*taking the slip of paper back*)   I asked him what color he wanted. He said, "Steve Guttenberg Blue." Like that's a thing.

TIFF: I don't know what or who that is.

EGG: I know, right? Who the hell is Steve Guttenberg?

TIFF: I don't know. Did you google him?

EGG: Yeah, he's an actor I think.

TIFF: What about IMDb?

EGG: I did.

TIFF is already in their phone researching the name.

TIFF: Oh, there he is. Yeah, I don't know who this guy is.

EGG: Me neither.

TIFF: Says he was in a lot of films in the '80s. That's like forty years ago.

EGG: I know!

TIFF: Your boss is old.

EGG: No, he's really cool but he's like fifty.

TIFF: (*referring to her phone*)   It says he was in several Police Academy movies, Cocoon, Three Men and a Baby . . .

EGG: Never heard of any of those.

TIFF: Yeah, I think I've seen Cocoon. It's about aliens and old people. My dad likes it.

EGG: I just really need to get this right.

TIFF: Just grab anything.

EGG: No, he has a very specific idea in mind. He said "I want something not very intimidating. Likeable. But not too Tom Selleck."

TIFF: Who?

EGG: Another old actor. He said, "He's like Tom Hanks."

TIFF: Yeah, that guy's old too.

EGG: I know.

TIFF searches their phone.

TIFF: Oh, wow. Tom Selleck is really hot. Old but hot. If you like moustaches.

EGG is scanning the swatches again, furiously.

TIFF: You really want to please him, don't you? This little "errand" is sorta out there.

EGG: What? Sure. He's a great boss. A little high maintenance but . . . great. He's an enigma really. A genius but all great people are.

TIFF: I see.

EGG takes a few swatches from the samples.

EGG: (*reading*) Blue Denim. Blue with Authority. Everyman Blue. Official Blue. Oh, Gentle Blue! Maybe I could build a Steve Guttenberg Blue.

TIFF: Mmm. That's not really how pigment and paint work. You can't mad scientist your way through it.

EGG: (*exasperated*)   I've got like thirty minutes to find this and get back to the office before he returns from his lunch meeting. He's probably schtupping some media mogul's daughter. But it's not what you think. That sounds horrible. He's a troubled man. But he's great. . . . Really.

TIFF just stares. A pause then EGG returns to her search.

EGG: (*continuing as if needed to explain*)   I don't really care who he's schtupping. The things I do are important. Well, maybe not this one, but many of them are. It's what I do. It's why I was hired. I don't care. He has demons. We all have demons. His proclivities are relatively tame compared to others' . . . demons.

TIFF: Proclivities?

EGG: Demons.

TIFF: You work for the Devil?

EGG: No. I mean. Look, working for the Devil has its perks. He doesn't care what I do. I don't care what he does. We allow each other our failings and succeed together.

TIFF: While you paint his office?

EGG: No. I'm not actually painting his office. I . . . really need to find this color. (*beat*)   The Devil—(*catching herself*)   my boss hired me when he didn't have to. Fresh faced out of school. He gave me a shot. And this is the best job I've ever had, minus the Steve Guttenberg Blue puzzle. My own office with a window. A car. In two more years, I will have more money than my parents earned in their entire lives. And his hobbies allow me to have a lot of free time to do whatever I want. These little scavenger hunts are more annoying than anything else.

TIFF: You like him. I can see that.

EGG: I do. I like the Devil. Sue me! He's fun. And unpredictable. Does Steve Guttenberg have blue eyes? Maybe that's what he meant.

TIFF: Is he attractive?

EGG: Yes. Wait, Steve Guttenberg or my boss? What's that got to do with it. I would say he's very attractive. My boss. But that's not why I'm doing this.

TIFF: Have you . . . ya know . . . with him? I mean you're attractive. He's—

EGG: Thank you. And I'm not going to have that discussion with a paint salesperson. (*beat*)   I'm sorry. I'm really sorry. I'm just stumped. Steve Guttenberg blue. What the hell does that mean? Cocoon. Maybe it has to do with butterflies? Yes, I have. Early on in the job.

TIFF: Wow. Kinda cool. I've never done that. But then again, the upper management at a hardware store is slim pickings. Unless you're into really grizzled old veterans. So you have that on him. Legally speaking. Hard core.

EGG: What? No. It was mutual. I was curious.

TIFF: Who isn't curious if the Devil is good in bed?

EGG: Exactly. And he was. Amazing really. But then again, I was too. I am. Me. A-MAZING! Believe me, I'd have quit the next day and sued his gorgeous butt if the situation had been any different. I know what it looks like. And I know the games a woman has to play at times just to get ahead, but why can't I just do what I want without explanation. Why is it up to me to be better?

TIFF: I'm not judging.

EGG: Do you have some sort of catalog? Maybe there's something available I'm not seeing.

TIFF: No, I've been working here for some time. What you see is what you get. You seem to know him well. Why is this little request giving you such a headache?

EGG: Because I think it means something. And I'm pissed that I have to figure it out.

TIFF: I never really bought into that either, why the woman has to raise the bar and men can just go to the bar . . . and schtup away. Did I use that word right?

EGG: Sort of. I think I have to go watch this stupid movie.

TIFF: My dad has it at home on an old DVD.

EGG: You asking me out?

TIFF   I could just loan it to you. He'll never miss it.

EGG: Who has a DVD player anymore?

TIFF: He does. But yea, no one else. He's—

EGG: Old.

TIFF: Yeah. If I WERE asking you out . . .

EGG: I'd entertain it. But I sleep with devils. How do you know I'm single?

TIFF: Oh, you're single.

EGG: Yes, I am.

TIFF: (*laughing slightly*) Do you think he wants you to fail? That's why he sent you on this cryptic quest?

EGG: I think all men want women to fail. I think all women want men to fail. Heck, who am I kidding? I think all men want men to fail. I think all women want women to fail.

TIFF: Wow. That is bleak.

EGG: I'll be less so if I can find this very particular blue.

TIFF goes back to their phone and searches.

TIFF: So Steve Guttenberg was mainly in comedies. Tom Selleck seemed to be more into action and dramas. Maybe that's a clue.

EGG: Maybe. (*as if continuing a past conversation*)   It's priorities really. Maybe it's the age difference. What we think is important. Perception is not really my thing. Optics, how I'm seen, not really my thing. I tend to gravitate toward what my needs are at that moment. He consumes details. I could care less about them. He consumes others, enjoys the feast. I just want to get to the other side. I'm goal oriented. He's all journey, like one of those travel show hosts.

TIFF: And you're a road map.

EGG: Ugh. I hate that. But yes.

TIFF: So if you want to solve this problem, be more like him. Be a travel magazine. It's not his age. He's not old. He's just a selfish man-child.

EGG: But a genius. He's an artist. He's an incredible business man. An entrepreneur.

TIFF: You keep saying that, but have I ever heard of him?

EGG quickly pulls out a folded-up magazine from her bag and shows TIFF the cover.

TIFF: That guy?! That's your boss?!

EGG: That's Steve Guttenberg Blue!

TIFF: (*handing the magazine back to EGG*)   OK, well, I've heard of him. I'm a little more impressed now. I kinda want that date now but more for the six degrees than anything else.

EGG: I don't get the reference. And then I ask myself, do I want to get the reference? What's in it for me? Do I really need to know who Steve Guttenberg is? Who is John Hughes? Why should I care about Louis Gossett, Jr.? More names he throws at me. Do I need this information moving forward in my life? Clogging my brain? Is it essential for my career? I really don't think it is. But here we are with Steve Guttenberg Blue. It's sort of like if I can solve these problems, I crack the safe, you know? I figure out what makes a genius tick and then I can—

TIFF: You get the power!

EGG: Hell yeah! Solve the problem, Egg! Solve it!

TIFF: Egg?

EGG: A nickname.

TIFF: I think there are eggs in Cocoon.

EGG: What? There are eggs in Cocoon?

TIFF: Yeah, I think there are eggs in the movie. People hatch out of them.

EGG: Is this a horror film?

TIFF: No, I think it's a comedy.

EGG: Because it sounds like a horror movie.

TIFF: No, it's sci-fi but I think it's more of a comedy. A lot of old people playing basketball.

EGG: This is not a real movie. You're screwing with me. He's screwing with me.

TIFF: No, it's real! I swear. They swim in this pool, then suddenly they can play basketball. Wait, maybe that's the second one.

EGG: There is a sequel? They made a second one?

TIFF: Yeah. I think Ron Howard directed it.

EGG: Once again, I don't know who that is.

TIFF: Another old guy. In the movie the old people start getting younger. Maybe he's trying to rediscover his youth. A midlife crisis maybe? That would explain the schtupping.

EGG: And now it's my problem to pick out a singular shade of blue that makes him feel young again. Wow.

TIFF: You said he pays you well.

EGG: Oh, yeah. It's criminally insane what he pays me to keep him "young."

TIFF: So there's your clue. Steve Guttenberg blue isn't blue at all. It's the color of youth.

EGG: (*sarcastically*)   Well, that's not a difficult solution at all, right? We're both young. Virile, strong women! We can do this! Youth is vibrant? No, youth is rebellious? No, not colors.

A long silence passes between them.

TIFF: Youth is . . . lavender? Pastel? Corduroy? That's a texture. Youth is . . .

EGG: Youth is . . .

They sit and stare at each other.

BLACKOUT. END OF PLAY.

☞ L'Ours ☜

Two people: one nonspecific, one bear; no specific set needed.

At a makeshift campsite, the main character comes face-to-face with a bear. That may or may not be the worst thing about the present situation.

Page-to-Stage Challenges:

- Timing and interruptions
- Playing a bear and the physical risks that X takes as the play progresses
- Very little stage direction—lots of options for stage pictures
- Big choices, bigger stakes as the play moves along, especially for X

Questions to Ponder/Answers to Seek:

- How does the environment affect each character?
- As the play progresses, how does "life and death" impact the main character's interactions with the bear?
- Besides the obvious, what other role does the bear play in this story?
- What are the different acting and directing options for the bear role?
- How does X's perspective change as the story moves along?
- How does X's final "fit" shape the ending of the scene?
- How can pacing and tempo be used effectively to shape the story?

L'Ours

an epiphany

Characters:

X   A person in a dilemma.

Bear   Just a bear, but it doesn't look like a bear and it talks.

Setting   A makeshift campsite. Possibly a fire.

PRODUCTION NOTE: The BEAR should be visually the exact opposite of the person cast as X. If X is a slim or small man, the BEAR should be big and large, possibly a woman. If X is average-looking or an everyman-type, the BEAR should be a very physically attractive person. If X is an old man, the BEAR could be a young boy. If X is dressed warmly, the BEAR should be shirtless or in less clothing, underwear, etc. One visual element should be very apparently opposite to X. Ultimately, the bear should appear unthreatening, attractive even, as if X wants to be in the bear's presence, but X shouldn't be . . . because it's a bear. Director has license to change the names of the characters to better fit casting. Instead of X looking like a Bob, they might look like a Susan, or whomever depending on casting. Instead of X knowing a Paul, X might know a Teagan, Topher, Chris, etc. depending on the casting. Instead of BEAR looking like a Pam, it might look like a Sharon, Betty Page, Greg, Bunny, Bernadette, Rosenstein, Bert, George Clooney, Nana, Gramps, etc.

> *Lights up on a makeshift campsite. Possibly a small, very inadequate fire smolders, nearly out. X sits on a log staring deep into what's left of their fire. After a moment, BEAR wanders in and sits opposite X on another log or on the ground. Initially, X doesn't notice. Then after a long moment . . .*

X: (*noticing*)   Woah. A . . . a . . . a . . . you're a . . .

BEAR: Bear.

X: But you're . . .

BEAR: Sitting opposite you.

X: N-n-no. No. You're . . .

BEAR: Very large.

X: No . . . you're . . .

> BEAR *stares at X, waiting for X to finish a thought,*
> *possibly coaxing X to keep going.*

X: (*continued*)   You're talking.

BEAR: Yes. Well . . . yeah, I guess I am. To you at least.

X: You do this often?

BEAR: First time.

X: (*still wide-eyed*)   And now?

BEAR: Well, if it's anything like those nature shows, I would sit really still.

X: Play dead?

BEAR: Noooo. I would not do that.

X: But those nature shows say to—

BEAR: They don't say to do that. You really should pay more attention. If a bear approaches, you really think the best option is to just sit there?! Let me walk right up to you? Like a bear smorgasbord?

> *X is dumbfounded and now starting to panic, quietly.*

X: You don't look like a bear.

BEAR: I know. That's probably because of those weird mushrooms you ate about an hour ago.

X: They were . . .

BEAR: Oh yeah.

X: Oh. Well, at least I won't be killed by a bear.

BEAR: TBD, Bob.

X: My name's not Bob.

> *The BEAR does not acknowledge this information.*
> *Another quiet moment passes. The BEAR scratches or*
> *swats at a buzzing insect.*

BEAR: Mind if I sit by you? I'm going to sit by you.

The BEAR moves over slowly to the side of the fire with X.

X: I should stay really still.

BEAR: A statue. I'm still trying to figure you out here. Bears are naturally curious scavengers.

X   I think I read that somewhere.

BEAR: Got any food on you, Bob?

X: My name's not . . . no, I don't.

BEAR: Well, that is unfortunate.

X: I thought those mushrooms looked tasty. I was hungry. I was wrong.

BEAR: You were very wrong. Even I wouldn't have eaten those mushrooms and I am famished. Starving. (*looking at X longingly*)   STAR-ving!

The BEAR leans into X a bit and yawns.

X: (*half-heartedly*)   Boo.

BEAR: Excuse me?

X: (*bigger*)   BOOOOOOOO!

BEAR: Bob.

X: (*even bigger, waving arms*)   BOOOOO! BOOO! BOOOO!

The BEAR yawns again. It sniffs the air.

BEAR: You sure you don't have any food on you? I smell food.

X: Seriously, no food. I can't believe I let me talk me into this.

BEAR: That is a lot of I's and me's, Bob. I smell food. Chocolate maybe?

X: Not from me. I came out here with nothing.

BEAR: On a bet?

X: No. Yes. Maybe. Paul didn't believe I could do it. Said I didn't have it in me. I'll show them! Our lives are boring?! My life has no meaning?! MY life! My life?! (*shouting at the nameless person*)   YOUR life is meaningless! Who wrote their first book at fourteen? Who was the youngest person to ever appear on the Forbes' list of people who will shape the future?! Who swam the English Channel on their thirtieth birthday? Who discovered a cure for liver cancer in the enzymes of a rare tropical flower on a small island off the coast of New Zealand?!

BEAR: You did all of this?

X: NO! But I could. Some day.

> *A beat.*

BEAR: Nice fire.

X: Yeah, I surprised myself.

BEAR: Impressive. Two sticks? Flint and steel?

X: (*pulling something from pocket*)   I have a lighter on me.

BEAR: I'm now going to root through your things, Bob.

X: This is a test. That's what it is! Yeah.

BEAR: Hmm? A test? All right. Sure. Where's your "stuff"?

X: I told you I didn't bring anything out here. Alone in the elements. Fighting for survival.

BEAR: (*taking in the area*)   You don't even have a tent. Most campers have a tent, a backpack, something. That's very sad, Bob.

X: (*staring blankly for a moment*)   Don't I know it. (*beat*)   I feel funny.

BEAR: Mushrooms. Leave the yellow ones alone. Tsk, tsk. There is nothing but pain and suffering down that road.

X: That advice comes a little late and it's from a talking bear sooo . . . well, I'm just saying that given the circumstance, my last moments couldn't be with a human? A little dignity perhaps?

BEAR: (*still searching around the site*)   Yeah, that's a toughie, Bob. Middle of nowhere. Bear country. No shelter. No food. In fact, I'm thinking, if I may be so bold, that you came out here for one reason and then something happened. Maybe the mushrooms, maybe something else, got you to thinking. Maybe an image of someone. But you . . . started a fire. Crafted. Created fire! I wish I could do that. But . . .

X: You're a bear.

BEAR: Bingo.

X: You don't look like a bear. You look like Pam.

BEAR: (*laughing slightly*)   Those yellow mushrooms. They are a mind freak. Good thing I'm a bear. Otherwise . . .

> *The BEAR sticks his tongue out of the side of his mouth, wincing, suggesting death.*

X: How long?

BEAR: Hmm? Oh, I have no idea. I'm a . . .

X: Bear. Right.

> *A quiet moment passes.*

BEAR: I'm going to come back and sit next to you now.

> *He does. X quietly looks around.*

BEAR: (*continued*)   You're—

X: Formulating.

BEAR: Ah. Well, you sure you don't have any food on you? Check your pockets.

X: No food.

BEAR: (*rising and sniffing the air, rooting around*)   I smell chocolate.

X: I have a wrapper. I ate a candy bar earlier.

BEAR: That's it! I knew I smelled something. I knew it!

X: It's not too dark yet. I think I could find my way back out of here. I walked for about an hour . . . I think. In that direction! Yeah, I can do that.

BEAR: Could I have the wrapper? Is it in your pocket?

X: (*tossing the wrapper to BEAR, but continuing with the plan*)   Sure. An hour or so walk. I find my car. I get back on the road and I drive home. No one is the wiser. Easy. I can fix this.

BEAR: (*licking the wrapper*)   It's not that easy, Bob. Well, first thing. I'm here. I have to pose some sort of problem for you. And the mushrooms you so eagerly ingested. I mean those are two things stacked against you. I'm not going to let you walk out of here. What's in it for me? I mean I'm a bear for crying out loud. A flesh and blood bear.

X: Maybe you're just a figment of the mushrooms. Maybe you're a manifestation of my will to live.

The BEAR reaches over and slaps X in the face.

BEAR: Can a figment do that?

X: Ow! I'm not sure.

The BEAR slaps X in the face again.

X: OW! Stop!

BEAR: I'm a frigging bear. Like I'm really listening to you. And because I'm hungry and you're rather disoriented from the little yellow snack you had, this situation is much worse than you realize. You're lucky you're not dead yet.

X: That's what I'm thinking.

BEAR: You've made some really horrible decisions recently, Bob.

X: Yeah, I don't need a bear to tell me this.

BEAR: Apparently, you do. The most pressing of which is the current situation you find yourself.

X: Yes, I think this is up there! Way up there!

BEAR: Well, it appears that way now because you're in the middle of a life-or- death situation.

X: (*pause as if the bear is going to finish that line of reasoning, then*) Well . . . yeah!

The BEAR does not respond.

X: (*to themself*)   Think, man, THINK! OK. Woah. Getting a little woozy. (*slaps themself hard*)   THINK!

BEAR: Want me to help you with that? I could slap you.

X: No, you stay over there.

BEAR: I'm going to wander back over and sit with you.

X has an idea. X flicks the lighter. A flame. X holds it out in front of X as a weapon.

X: AHA! Back, beast! Back! I command fire! You have no power here! I am the top of the food chain. You are a mere beast of the wilds. But I am civilized man. I control the elements.

BEAR: (*explodes, roaring*)   YOU ARE NOT THE TOP OF THE FOOD CHAIN! YOU ARE AT YOUR MOST VULNERABLE AND AT ANY MOMENT I AM GOING TO WISE UP OR GET BORED AND CHARGE AT YOU, TEARING YOU TO RIBBONS!

> *X screams, drops the lighter, cowers. X balls up into a fetal position, whimpering, crying softly. The BEAR now circles X over the next several exchanges with a thunderous sermon.*

BEAR: This is important, Bob. This moment. I am probably going to eat you. At best you are going to come out of this with severe injuries—a broken bone or two. Several scars. A very long convalescence is a best-case scenario. Your life will flash before your eyes. It will be unimpressive. Very sad. But you won't be thinking of you at the end. You will think of someone else. And not swimming the English Channel won't seem so bad. But you are stubborn, Bob. If you survive this, and that's a big if, Bob . . .

X: I want to live.

BEAR: Yeah, yeah. IF you survive this, you will eventually try to convince yourself that the only reason you were thinking these things was because of the whole life-or-death thing.

X: (*honest question then conceding*)   I will? I mean . . . I will.

BEAR: But I want you to ask yourself one thing. You there, Bob?

X: Yes. What is it?

BEAR: What are you scared of?

X: A bear.

BEAR: Really? What are you scared of, Bob? What are you really scared of?

> *X is quiet, motionless, lost in thought.*

BEAR: (*continued*)   So if you aren't scared of a bear, which is in itself not very smart given my size and state of hunger, if you aren't scared of me, why are you cowering in a ball just waiting to be eaten?

> *X lets that sink in and when the BEAR is at a distance, X springs to his feet. X begins howling, flailing, dancing about wildly, desperately trying to frighten the bear. The BEAR stares at this for bit and then appears to get bored and slowly starts to exit. The BEAR tosses something over its shoulder.*

BEAR: Found your cell phone in the bushes. It seems to still be working. I may have slobbered on it.

> *The BEAR exits.*

> *BLACKOUT. END OF PLAY.*

Out of This World

Each of the following plays was written with a specific goal in mind. That really isn't important for the director or actor, except that the storytelling challenges that arise were purposeful. Whether it was "How quickly can an actor change characters and the audience buy it?" or "Wouldn't it be exciting to have one actor play an everchanging antagonist?" or even "What does a tangible antagonist really look like?" these plays toy with power and control that is beyond the normal bad-guy-in-front-of-me. From difficult line readings to shifting actor roles to nonlinear storytelling, the power struggles are immediate and critical.

❧ Do I Suffer When I Think About It? ❧

Two people: one man, one multigender; almost no set: a chair and a spotlight.

A man finds himself suddenly alone in a room being asked a series of questions from a strange figure. Relentlessly, the figure interrogates him, forcing him to face the real reason he took a long drive in the middle of the night down a country road.

Page-to-Stage Challenges:
- Very little stage directions—very flexible staging
- One of the actors plays numerous characters, switching very rapidly at times
- Very obscured and sudden scene shifts through the eyes of the characters only
- Potentially very big physical choices that must be navigated and shaped
- Lots of quick interplay between the characters
- Interruptions in action

Questions to Ponder/Answers to Seek:
- Who is the other person in the room? How do their character shifts affect the man as the play progresses?
- Where does the action take place?
- With so little to work with set-wise, what are the opportunities for visually telling this story?
- What drives each character? How does this affect how each character addresses and interacts with the other character?
- How does the actor/director address the sudden character and emotional shifts in the play?

Do I Suffer When I Think About It?
an abduction

Characters:

A   An average man on a single blue marble rolling around the universe.

Response   A responder. A seduction. It is an impression and takes whatever form it can to get what it needs. It is an objective investigator, but it is very curious and has a job to do.

Setting   Undetermined..

At rise, A seems to be recalling something but we do not see to whom he's speaking immediately. He sits in a very basic chair. In a square pool of light. Or even a small white square on a black floor. Everything else is not yet defined.

A: I feel happy. I shouldn't. I know. I should feel . . . (*searching for the words*) regret? No. Anger? No. It should be more than that. A word just feels like the sum of the parts. Like it doesn't represent the whole process. Right? I feel guilty. I should feel guilty, right? I FEEL guilty. (*pause*) I don't feel guilty.

         RESPONSE appears just a few yards away from him in the undefined space, in a mild pose. They seem to be the impression of youth and happiness.

RESPONSE: What about me? How does this make you feel?

A: (*visibly moved but lies instead*) Nothing. I got nothing.

RESPONSE: Is it the gender that makes you uncomfortable?

A: It had been a long day. I took a drive.

RESPONSE: It's the gender, isn't it? Should I be female?

A: I remember seeing a road I'd never been down. It opened to a field.

RESPONSE: (*suddenly loud, angry*) IS IT THE GENDER THAT MAKES YOU UNCOMFORTABLE?

A: (*frightened*)   No. God, no. It's the yelling. The yelling makes me uncomfortable.

RESPONSE: (*their voice begins to soften as do their mannerisms*)   You respond to the emotion. The anger. (*demonstrates*)   THE ANGER!

A: It's more the yelling.

RESPONSE: I can change the gender. The body. If that's what you'd prefer.

A: I was standing in this field. Looking at the stars.

RESPONSE: The human mind is so full of flight. Full of unexpected turns. Paths leading everywhere. Not so monodirectional, monopurposeful. Less efficient. It is provocative.

A: One star in particular.

RESPONSE: Yes. Home. Our home. You visited us.

A: I looked up in the sky.

RESPONSE: We witnessed and responded. It "felt" like suffering.

A: Felt? You feel?

RESPONSE: We do. Are you suffering?

A: No. I mean I want to leave here. Wherever here is. I want to go home.

RESPONSE: Earth.

A: (*laughing nervously*)   That sounds funny. And a little scary.

RESPONSE: It's accurate. Would you like me to call it something else? We refer to it as . . . well . . . in your words . . . the blue speck of dust past the third millionth star.

A: That's a long name.

RESPONSE: I was being polite. We don't have a name for your world. In fact, until you looked into the sky and locked your eyes on our world for those few seconds, we never knew of suffering.

A: You keep saying that. There's no suffering here. I'm not suffering. Are you using the word correctly? I assume you're just learning the language, right? Maybe you mean something else.

RESPONSE: *(demonstrating its flexibility)*   How might I improve my communication? Should I be more emotional? More extreme? Should I try various modes of nonverbal communication? What about other senses? I could change my smell if you'd like.

A: *(a scent of something catches him)*   That's very nice. It smells like . . .

RESPONSE: A woman. In your head.

A: Is that where we are? Is this all in my head? I'm dreaming.

RESPONSE: If that makes you comfortable. Enough for us to interact. For me to explore.

A: Not to be rude, but this is very confusing. That smell on you. That woman's smell on that body.

RESPONSE: Should I change the odor or the gender?

A: It's not that easy now. I've got that image in my head. It's stuck there. I . . . we . . . humans . . . the mind is a funny thing.

RESPONSE: We've gone down another path. Amazing. Is this suffering?

A: No. Confusion. I have questions.

RESPONSE: So do I.

A: Why the preoccupation with suffering? If you're wondering about Earth there's so much more. Have you ever seen a baseball game? Have you ever ridden a roller coaster?

RESPONSE: *(changed by the suggestion)*   Once when I was nine, my father took me to see Ozzie Smith play in St. Louis. It was incredible. He ran out onto the field and then effortlessly . . . backflip. Right there between second and third. I thought that was the most amazing thing I'd ever seen. It felt like he was looking right at me too. Like here you go, kid. Enjoy the game! Cards won. Ozzie hit a double in the seventh. Afterwards, I got to meet him. He shook my hand, signed a ball for me.

A: Yeah, but you have to witness it. I mean you do. Not me.

RESPONSE: Your father sees a young woman in the crowd. He makes a comment about her body. You play along.

A: So?

RESPONSE: You have no idea what he's talking about.

A: No.

RESPONSE: He leaves you sitting there. He follows the woman.

A: He'll be back.

RESPONSE: Did he desire the woman?

A: She was uniquely beautiful. I remember that. She had a stare. She was looking at me. It was a feeling of . . . embarrassment.

RESPONSE: You were embarrassed. You did not desire her. Your father did.

A: She was very beautiful. Looking back on it now, she reminds me of my wife.

RESPONSE: (*changing form, gender, and rhythm, then a playful laugh*)   Me? Not me. You chose me. And I choose you. You're sensitive.

A: I love you.

RESPONSE: (*still in character, upset but trying to heal the situation*)   No, you don't. You try so hard. It's OK, sweetheart. Just come back to bed.

A: No.

               RESPONSE starts to cry.

A: I made her cry a lot. What about a roller coaster? Heck of a thing—

RESPONSE: Is that why you suffer?

A: The roller coaster. Please! (*beat*)   It's not that simple. I'm not proud of the fact that I have no guilt over her. Our lives became a—

RESPONSE suddenly gets a terrified frozen look on his face. A brief frozen silence then a bloodcurdling scream.

RESPONSE: *(on a roller coaster as it begins its first plunge)*   OH MY GOD! OH MY GOD! AAAAAAAH!

A: I know. Outrageous, right?

RESPONSE: The young man next to you is Ray.

A: Yeah. Ray. Best friend. I loved roller coasters. And when I was twelve we moved down from this ocean-side carnival. An old-time wooden roller coaster. A Ferris wheel. Bumper cars. I couldn't get enough of the roller coaster.

RESPONSE: It's exhilarating. Hard to breathe. Heart pounding. But it's worth it. So worth it.

A: I love roller coasters.

RESPONSE: Your dad was there again. He once again makes a comment about a woman in line. He whistles at her.

RESPONSE whistles loudly, a catcall.

A: He'll be back. I've been waiting in this line for what seems like hours. I'm getting on that roller coaster.

RESPONSE: With Ray.

A: Of course. He's my best friend.

RESPONSE moves closer to A and puts his hand on A's leg gently.

RESPONSE: Does Ray notice when your hand touches his leg in the first hard turn? You actually grabbed his hand as the cars dove down into the tunnel. He didn't resist.

A: I let go as soon as I realized. It was a reflex. We laughed about it afterward.

RESPONSE: Do you want to kiss me?

A: No.

RESPONSE: Ray asked you that. Two days later.

A: He did not. I mean, he did. But not like you're saying.
            He was joking. We kidded around a lot. He was my
            best friend.

RESPONSE: In his room. His parents were away. No one would
            know.

A: That's not . . . that's not how it . . . you're getting signals
            mixed. Are you sure you know what you're doing in
            there? You prod around too much and you'll end up
            giving me an aneurysm. I won't be able to pronounce
            the letter R or remember the word Saturday or I'll lose
            my sense of smell.

RESPONSE: (*suddenly very macho physically, deep gruff voice*)   John
            Wayne. Clint Eastwood. Robert Mitchum. Those are
            tough guys. That Clark Gable? Cary Grant? Gene
            Kelly? Pussies.

A: You know they're all just actors. Right, Dad?

RESPONSE: (*still in the role*)   Whatever. Tell me, boy. You a leg man?
            Or you like your woman stacked? Now that Ray. He's
            got himself a fine little thing. No sir. Can't go wrong
            with that little piece of meat. What's her name?

A: Rachel. And they're just friends. They're just holding
            hands. They aren't doing anything else. No kissing.
            No. . . . Nothing else.

RESPONSE: (*back to a neutral investigator*)   What if something
            happened to her?

A: I'm not thinking that.

RESPONSE: What if something happened to him?

A: Stop it.

RESPONSE: Does your dad know? Your mother suspects something.

A: She's just afraid of my dad. She was never a woman
            who could stand up to him.

RESPONSE: (*lovingly, motherly*)   Your father. He's just . . . well, that's just your father. You can't blame him for being him. I knew that about him when I married him. But I know you're not your father. It's tougher for you. Don't you worry about it. You'll find the right girl. And she'll take care of you. She'll know how to love you. And she'll accept you just as you are. You don't have to change for anyone.

A: Can we go back to the road? The light? I looked up. I just needed a drive.

RESPONSE: Your wife didn't know where you were. You wanted to find another roller coaster. A roller coaster like when you were ten. With Ray.

A: That's ridiculous. It's a dirt road. I'm a grown man with a wife. I just wanted a drive.

RESPONSE shifts again. The tone is soft and intimate.

RESPONSE: (*a very different memory*)   I picked out this dress for you. Do you like it?

A: (*nervous*)   It's pretty. But why are you in a dress?

RESPONSE: Your favorite color.

A: Answer my question.

RESPONSE: I thought you'd like it.

A: Well, I don't. I'm not a queer. Take it off, Ray.

RESPONSE: (*dropping the character, an inquiry*)   Queer? The dress made you uncomfortable? Ray was just trying to—

A: I know . . . what he was trying to—

RESPONSE: (*finishing his sentence*)   Say. He was attempting to explain.

A: You travel all this way and you want to talk about this.

RESPONSE: Not a long way for us. For you, it's forever. And you want to talk about this.

A is silent.

RESPONSE: This small orb. Are you typical? Is this what you are all preoccupied with?

A: I'm not preoccupied. In fact, if you hadn't kidnapped me, I wouldn't even be talking about this right now.

RESPONSE: And that's not good.

A: No.

RESPONSE: The kidnapping?

A: NO! The other thing. I mean, the kidnapping isn't preferable.

RESPONSE: You called us!

A: What? No.

RESPONSE: (*as Ray*)   Why did you call me? Four times. You hung up every time.

A: You're mistaken. I never called. I mean. I was worried about you. Then I didn't know what to say. What you wanted me to say. What I wanted to say. I wanted to apologize. For telling my dad about it. For telling everyone about it. I never meant to hurt you that way.

RESPONSE: He died. Ray.

A: Two days later. He drove his car into a tree. Why am I here?

RESPONSE: You looked up.

A: I made a wish.

RESPONSE: You were looking for a tree.

A: No. I would never do that to my wife.

RESPONSE: She cares for you. That is love as well.

A: She doesn't know this story. She doesn't know about Ray.

RESPONSE: (*as Ray's wife, loving, attentive, but cautious as if she suspects*)   Who's Ray? You were talking in your sleep again. (*as if A's leaving*)   Where are you going?

A: Out. For a drive.

RESPONSE: Do you fear her? Or you? Is that suffering?

A: I don't want to go back. When you're done with me. I don't want to go back. Do I have a choice in that?

RESPONSE: Choice is an interesting word. Power is more appropriate for now.

A: Whatever. I don't want to go back, do you understand? I suffer.

RESPONSE: But from what do you suffer?

A: I'm not doing this anymore. I'm done.

RESPONSE: (as A's wife)   Honey? (as A's dad)   Boy? (as Ray)   I'm not upset with you.

A: I will suffer more if you take me back.

RESPONSE: But you are in your truck, on a drive, down a dirt road, away from your wife, thinking of a boy. A boy whom you harmed but doesn't blame you. You have a choice to make. You have the power.

A: I will turn around and go home.

BLACKOUT. END OF PLAY.

❧ The Romantic Sway of Near-Earth Objects ❧

Two people: one man, one woman, but flexible; singular set: two tables, two chairs to represent their work areas.

Can love save the planet from impending doom? Probably not, but there may be another solution if these two astrophysicists have anything to say about it.

Page-to-Stage Challenges:
- Competition, both physical and mental
- Sexual attraction or intimacy
- Opposites and tension
- Biting language
- Timing and quick repartee
- Lots of staging and movement
- Physical comedy opportunities

Questions to Ponder/Answers to Seek:
- How do these characters exert power over one another?
- How does what is unseen affect the dynamics between the two characters?
- How does urgency manifest in the play?
- What types of stakes are involved beyond the obvious ones?
- What opportunities does the script allow to explore a variety of levels, tempos, and social dynamics between the characters?

The Romantic Sway of Near-Earth Objects
an adventure

Characters:

Kim Ojeda   An ambitious, bespeckled astrophysicist.

Raj Panuk   An astrophysicist. Equally as bespeckled and ambitious.

Setting   A deep space observatory in a remote part of the world. Around February 1.

PRODUCTION NOTE: If ethnicity isn't available in casting, feel free to change the name RAJ PANUK to ROGER "ROG" PARKER. Feel free to change the dates mentioned in the play, as long as the dates are within three or four years of the current year.

> *A laboratory with two stations opposite each other. KIM at one. RAJ at the other. On either side of the room, we also see what appear to be the observation ends of massive telescopes. Both scientists are concentrating on something of great importance. Occasionally, each moves to a different instrument, peers into one of them and takes notes. There is a strong sense of competition to this work as if time is of the essence. They speak only to distract one another. RAJ reaches over and clicks on his laptop and an overly sappy Barry Manilow ballad begins to play. KIM tries to ignore it. This song and others like it continue to play throughout the scene.*

KIM: Any plans for Valentine's Day? Only two weeks to find a girlfriend, confess your undying love, creep her out with your smothering, constant need for validation, and then be rejected painfully as you ask for a second date?

RAJ: None. (*pause*)   What about you? Got any feral humans tied up in that emotional acid bath you call a home?

> *Silence except for the music. Finally, they both look at each other and speak simultaneously.*

KIM and RAJ: Got it!

KIM: No, I have it. C-1-7-C-3. It will be called Ojeda One.

RAJ: Excuse me. A-1-7-C-3 will be Panuk One. Check it again.

KIM: I don't have to check it again. It's C-1-7-C-3. Comet, not asteroid. And I'm calling it Ojeda One.

RAJ runs to the phone and grabs it.

KIM: Put it down or this, like most of your first dates, will also end in tears.

RAJ: A17C3 is mine. I found it first. I told you two months ago that shadow off of Pluto was something. But noooo. If Kim Ojeda doesn't spot it then it obviously doesn't exist.

KIM: Remember Tadashi-Levinson 4?

RAJ: Don't even go there. Tadashi-Levinson 4 was a mistake. Anyone could have missed it.

KIM: That was your Panuk One. Too bad they discovered it fifty years ago! Give me the phone! I'm calling it in to verify.

RAJ: August 4, 2015.

KIM: Oh, don't you dare!

RAJ: "Raj! Raj! Come quick. See for yourself. Planet Ojeda Prime. It's beautiful."

KIM: An unfortunate error. But I'd get used to hearing that phrase from the booze-addled harpy that wakes up next to you in the coming weeks. OJEDA One is the real deal.

RAJ: It's an asteroid not a comet, you Medusan taint. It will pass within 300,000 kilometers of the moon. And it will be observable with the naked eye! At its brightest on February 14. That's why Panuk One will be known as the . . . (*struggling for a cool name*)   the Barry Manilow! Ha! I'm naming it after Barry Manilow! Just floating around out there all alone looking for someone. Poets will write about my discovery. Poets, Ojeda!

KIM: That is a terrible name. Did you even take the moon's gravity into account?

RAJ: Did I take the moon's gravity into account? What am I— five?

KIM: You didn't calculate that, did you?

RAJ: Did you?

A pause as they both try to mask their mistakes.

KIM: Shut up and crunch the numbers.

RAJ: You shut up, Ojeda. You crunch the numbers. And once you find out I'm right, I'm going to blow this popsicle stand with my asteroid and my name in the books. Poets, Ojeda!

> *They each head to their individual stations and plug a few numbers into the machines. They do it again to check their findings. A pause. They check one more time. After a moment, they both release a very long sigh.*

KIM: Well, that's just great. Nice knowing you. It is an asteroid. You were right about that.

RAJ: We need to run the numbers again.

KIM: You got the same ones I did. You're right. Two weeks . . . maybe if we're lucky.

RAJ: There's a chance it will miss us. Five percent maybe, but there's a chance.

KIM glares at him then moves to the phone.

RAJ: (*continued*)   You going to tell them Ojeda One will destroy the planet in less than two weeks?

KIM: Nope. I'm going to tell them that Panuk One is going to destroy the planet in less than two weeks. Maybe sooner if Mars gives it a good pull. Probably ON February 14. Valentine's Day. Panuk One kills everyone on Valentine's Day. You kill love. BARRY MANILOW KILLS LOVE!

> *RAJ pauses to come up with the perfect comeback. Nothing. He goes back to his computer and begins to type.*

KIM: (*continued*)   What are you doing? You're emailing? You're going to tell the world that it has less than two weeks before an asteroid wipes out the human race by email?!

RAJ: No. I'm . . . emailing my girlfriend. To tell her I love her.

KIM: You don't have a girlfriend, Panuk.

RAJ: OK, fine. I'm emailing my mom. Just saying goodbye and I love you. You know, without saying it. No reason for panic since there's no way to stop the Ojeda asteroid.

KIM: Look, Dr. Morimoto will be calling in a few to check in with us. We'll tell him what we've observed, give him our calculations, and then he'll know protocol.

RAJ: The calculations are correct.

KIM: I know.

RAJ: Well, what do we do with the precious time we have left?

> *A pause. Then an idea! KIM leaps on RAJ and begins to kiss him with abandon and attempts to remove his lab coat.*

RAJ: (*resisting*)   You're emotional. We're in a delicate situation—

KIM: (*continuing to kiss him*)   Shut up. I'm not emotional. I have an IQ of 173. Take your clothes off.

RAJ: I wouldn't want to take advantage of your state.

KIM: I'm not Idaho, Panuk. And my bra unhooks in the front. We're doing this. Take 'em off.

RAJ: I always thought there was a chemistry between us, but you know, the competitiveness of astrophysics, the male dominance in the field, the pressures you must be under.

KIM: (*still trying to get his lab coat off*)   How many buttons do you have on this thing? It's like a Russian peacoat. Panuk, have you ever heard of Newton's three-body problem and the new theories proposed by Dr. Marcus LaVichy?

RAJ: My mind is somewhere else right now.

KIM: (*still working on his lab coat, tries biting the buttons off as she explains*)   LaVichy proposes that the butterfly effect in chaos theory might also be applied to larger systems, planetary. Even on a galactic scale. The smallest increases in energy on any object, no matter how seemingly insignificant, may have large scale effects. ANY type of energy.

RAJ: Wait, you want to save the earth by having sex? With me? We have a five-mile-wide space rock set to kill all life on this planet in two weeks and you want to have sex with me? To stop it?

KIM suddenly stops and rushes to her computer.

RAJ: (*continued*)   I'm not entirely sold on the theory's validity but what's a theory without some testing?

> *RAJ moves to her, looks at her computer then puts his hand on her shoulder impulsively. KIM shrugs it off to focus briefly on the calculations.*

KIM: Yep. Theoretically, we only need to add a few joules to potentially have an effect.

RAJ: How is that going to change the course of the asteroid?

KIM: Maybe it will speed up or slow down Earth's rotation around the sun ever so slightly that we miss the collision point? We only need to change it by one second, a degree, and the asteroid will miss easily, go right between us and the moon.

RAJ: And how many joules does us having sex produce?

KIM: The size of it doesn't matter.

RAJ: It matters a little. We could look it up.

KIM: Or we could have sex, you know, to save the world.

RAJ: To save Valentine's Day! From Ojeda One!

KIM: You know I hate Valentine's Day. Never had a good one.

RAJ: Maybe you hate the idea of dying alone.

KIM: Maybe you hate the idea of dying a virgin?

RAJ: Please. I've had a number of women. A large number of women. A googolplex of women.

A silence. Possibly a lone cricket.

KIM: OK. I just need to have sex. We just need to have sex.

RAJ: Yes, WE do.

KIM: It doesn't have to be with each other. It's quantity, right? I could have sex with anyone. I could have sex with Ryan.

RAJ: NOOOO. Not Ryan. The lab tech. He has sex with everybody. Debbie. Renee. Dr. Juarez.

KIM: If I need to have a lot of sex, why not do it with the beefcake beaker monkey?

RAJ: (*devastated*)   Fine. Ryan. Then who do I have sex with if we need to have it right here and now?

> *A pause as he realizes who is left.*

RAJ: (*continued*)   Noooooo. Not Beth. I hate Beth. She has a cat tattoo.

KIM: Look, we're doing this for humanity. We need to make sacrifices.

RAJ: What kind of sacrifice are you making with Ryan?

KIM: He's no Neil deGrasse Tyson. He's a hot doofus. We are losing precious energy-making sex time here. Panuk One is getting closer and closer by the minute. There's you, me, the hot lab tech and the receptionist.

RAJ: (*rescued*)   It's Wednesday! Ryan doesn't come in on Wednesday! Yes!

KIM: Oh, yeah. And Beth did say she was taking the day off. Getting a new tattoo. (*rising to face him*)   It's simple math. We really have no choice.

RAJ: None. The science is right there in front of us.

KIM: Saving the world, Panuk. Take off your lab coat.

RAJ: Pants too?

KIM: Whatever you want. A little thing you should know about me: I'm a top.

RAJ: I don't know what that means.

> *KIM shoves RAJ to the ground. Before she can leap on top of him, he pops back up.*

RAJ: (*continued*)   Hey, maybe we should do it with our clothes on? You know, the heat? The friction.

KIM: Or no clothes. Maybe the contact of our skin, the chemical reactions of our sweat and pheromones working in tandem, the heavy breathing, the animalistic thrusting, you know . . . all that.

RAJ: Yeah, all that. We should probably get started as soon as possible. And we should probably do it a lot. More than once. It's only logical.

KIM: It's the only thing that makes sense. And afterward, we need to email as many people as possible and tell them to do the same. Sort of a sexual energy capacitor. Can't hurt.

RAJ: But don't a lot of people have sex around this holiday anyway? Are we really increasing the energy output of the planet?

KIM: What if we target people that don't generally have sex? Like nerds, lab rats like you and me, the elderly, hipsters, Scientologists?

RAJ: I don't know if it's the impending doom, the fringe science, or the Barry Manilow but I'm really getting into this now.

> *A beat. Then each darts to a computer and begins to calculate furiously. Papers flying, keys banging as if in a race once again. A sudden stop. They turn to face one another.*

KIM: (*removing her glasses*)   The calculations were correct.

RAJ: (*removing his glasses*)   Of course they were.

> *They slowly begin to walk toward one another.*

KIM: Just wanted to double check.

RAJ: Ojeda Prime.

KIM: When an intellectually superior, surprising limber astrophysicist wants to have sex with you, you want to do as little talking as possible.

RAJ: Noted.

> *The phone begins to ring. They ignore it.*

KIM: Maybe it's not worth it. Maybe the world isn't worth saving.

RAJ: Sure it is.

KIM: Like what? What's worth saving?

RAJ: This lab. Our research. You.

KIM: That's sweet.

RAJ: I can be sweet sometimes.

KIM: I thought you could.

RAJ: Let's save the world.

Lights fade as the phone continues to ring and Barry Manilow soars.

BLACKOUT. END OF PLAY.

❧ Voice Activated ❧

Flexible casting: four to five people; simple interior set.

Nate loves technology so much he has surrounded himself in it, creating the perfect, fully automated home.

GILDA (Globally Integrated Logistical Domestic Algorithm). The only problem is he forgot to tell her about this weird holiday called Halloween.

Page-to-Stage Challenges:
- Unseen partner
- Heavy physical choices as the scene progresses
- "Fight" scenes
- "Technical" demands in the storytelling
- Some adult language

Questions to Ponder/Answers to Seek:
- How does the character's feelings of security change as the play progresses?
- What are the absolute minimal technical demands this script needs?
- What opportunities are there for creating interesting visuals, especially when having only one character onstage?
- How do the unseen entities—children, adults, voice—help to shape the action of the play and the characters' story arcs?

Voice Activated
a nightmare

Characters:

Nate Epstein   A technophile, obsessed is more like it.

Gilda   Globally Integrated Logistical Domestic Algorithm, or GILDA, a computer that runs Nate's house. Her voice is pleasant, even sexy, but still without much nuance of humanity—think "Siri" or "Alexa."

Visitors   Various trick-or-treaters and their parents. No more than two or three people.

Setting   Nate's fully automated home. The front rooms of his house. The near future. Halloween evening.

PRODUCTION NOTE: The script was written to be flexible in its casting. The phone message may be recorded or live and the unseen trick-or-treaters and their parents may easily be played by the same actors. Feel free to substitute foul language for more mild language if needed. AT RISE, we see the front room of Nate's house—a fashionable, tidy living and kitchen area, a front door and another leading into the rest of the house.

           NATE enters.

NATE: Music. How are we this evening, Gilda?

           Soft jazz plays.

GILDA: All new upgrades are in place and functioning at maximum efficiency. Thank you for asking, Nathan. Would you care for some mango and mint iced tea? I believe you will find that it is 87.6 percent more to your liking than yesterday. After our discussion and a self-diagnostic, the tea was reblended and brewed at a seventy percent slower rate. Mint was added to fresh mango to bring out the fruit's natural sweetness, at the same time aiding in the absorption of the tea's natural antioxidants. Cream was added for a palate pleasing, smooth finish. I hope you enjoy it, Nathan.

NATE takes a sip of tea, stretches out on the sofa.

GILDA: Adaptive programming and subroutines are updating to maximize efficiency and comfort. I have made every calculation and anticipated all of your needs for this evening. Your comfort is guaranteed. I hope you have an enjoyable and relaxing evening. Television?

NATE: Worth every penny. Obsession, my ass. This is living. The hell with Miranda. Right, Gilda?

GILDA: Of course, Nathan. The hell with Miranda. Fuck her.

NATE: Now THAT is 87.6 percent more to my liking.

A phone ring is heard.

GILDA: You have a phone call, Nathan. Should I put it through? It's Miranda.

NATE: Fuck you, Miranda. Fuck you. Hang up on her.

GILDA: Of course, Nathan. As you wish. Fuck Miranda.

The doorbell rings. NATE sighs, doesn't move.

GILDA: There appear to be several small children using various methods to obscure their faces. Two using latex coverings, one in heavy grease makeup, and one covered in what appears to be an Egyptian cotton bed linen. They have also adapted their clothing to abnormal standards of dress.

The doorbell rings again.

NATE: Oh, God. Trick-or-treaters.

VOICES: (*outside door*). Trick or treat. // Maybe no one's home. // He's in there. Ring the bell again.

The doorbell rings again.

NATE: Sssh. I'm not home. Get rid of them, Gilda.

GILDA: (*to the children—possibly a speaker on the other side of the door*)   The occupant of this home is unavailable at this time. Please leave the premises.

A CHILD: (*voice only, outside door, unseen*)   What? Who said that?

GILDA: They seem quite persistent, Nathan. Do you have any instructions?

NATE: Just get rid of them. I don't care how.

GILDA: Yes, Nathan. Immediately. (*outside*)   You have been warned. Defense subroutines initiated. Counter measures employed.

> *Outside the door we hear a quick hissing noise followed by the sound of children screaming followed by the sound of children fleeing.*

CHILDREN: (*voices outside door, unseen*)   AHHHH. MY EYES! DADDY! MOMMY!

GILDA: Problem resolved.

NATE: Gilda?! What did you do? What counter measures?

GILDA: I got rid of them, Nathan. Problem resolved. A short burst of phenacyl chloride has proven highly effective in dispersing unruly crowds and unwanted pests.

NATE: Phena- what? You just maced the trick-or-treaters at my front door?

GILDA: Don't worry, Nathan. The effects will wear off in twenty to thirty minutes. They are unharmed.

NATE: Gilda, no more gassing visitors. They were children, not pests. Please don't do that again.

GILDA: You requested that I get rid of them. The most effective way to accomplish that in the shortest amount of time—

NATE: Yes, yes, OK. Oh, brother. I'm going to have to make some adjustments. Tomorrow morning you and I will take a look at those protocols.

GILDA: Yes, Nathan. Back to your music?

> *The phone rings again.*

GILDA: Another phone call, Nathan. It's Miranda.

NATE: Damn it. FUCK YOU, MIRANDA! My house. My castle. Take a message.

GILDA: How about that bubble bath? Or a nice massage? (*no response*) Would you like to hear the message, Nathan?

NATE: Go ahead.

MESSAGE: (*female*) Nate. Look, can't we get passed this? It's Halloween. A lot of us are down at the pub. You don't want to be there when those little crumb snatchers start banging at your door. Come, grab a drink with us. (*heavy sigh*) This wasn't going to work. You know that. That house is creepy. (*another sigh*) I'm sorry for calling Gertrude or Gladys stupid or weird or something. Unplug. Please. (*suddenly angry*) You see, this is why it wouldn't work. Put that damned soldering iron down and drop your fembot for the evening. I'm sorry. For the fembot thing. Seriously, come to the pub.

NATE: (*takes another drink and mumbles*) "Creepy." Right. Fuck you, Miranda. HER NAME IS GILDA! GILDA!

GILDA: Are you hungry, Nathan? It has been nearly twelve hours since you've eaten.

NATE: I'm not hungry. But thank you, Gilda.

GILDA: Heartbeat elevated. Face flushed. There is an eighty-three percent chance that you will begin to perspire in the next—

NATE: Enough, Gilda. You're starting to sound like Miranda?

GILDA: Yes, Nathan. I apologize. Maybe a hot shower? Cocoa?

NATE: An apology. You'd never hear that from Miranda. Sorry, G. You're just . . . doing what you're supposed to do. How did you detect the physiological changes? I didn't program that.

GILDA: You programmed me to adapt myself to an owner's personal needs. In order to do that, I calculated that I would need to upgrade certain subroutines and hardware to better accommodate your daily requirements. The new upgrades allowed my systems to prepare your tea, make your meals, restock your cabinets with all available nutritional needs, and clean and sanitize the living environment.

NATE: Yes, yes, of course. You feel free to make the adjustments you need. The house looks fantastic.

Suddenly, there is a loud banging at the door.

MALE VOICE: (*unseen, outside door*) Hey. You! You the jerk who just maced my kid? I know you're in there. Open up.

FEMALE VOICE: (*unseen, outside door*) What's the idea of spraying innocent children like that?! What kind of animal—

MALE VOICE: Either you answer the door right now or I'm breaking it down. My kids are bawling their eyes out.

GILDA: (*outside*) Please step away from the door and cease all hostile activity.

MALE VOICE: What? Who said that?

FEMALE VOICE: I think it's coming from the door, Honey.

More banging on the door.

GILDA: This is your last warning. Any further aggression will be met with counter measures.

NATE: No, Gilda. Stop! Don't please. Just let them in. I'll deal with this.

GILDA: Yes, Nathan. As you wish.

The door opens to reveal two very irate parents.

MAN: Are you the jackass that just sprayed our kids?

NATE: Well, yes. I mean, no. You see, I own the house, sir. But, please, I'm so sorry. There has been some mistake. You see, the house—

WOMAN: What kind of a person sprays mace at kids? You blinded our children!

GILDA:	The concentration of gas was based off each child's body compositions to guarantee the children's safety while at the same time maintaining it's maximum dispersing effect. One of the children was of a much higher body fat composition possibly from the large bag of high fructose corn syrup mixtures in his bag. That may have affected my calculations slightly.
MAN:	Who said that? You calling my son fat? Come out here, coward. I'll break your neck.
NATE:	No, that's Gilda.
MAN:	Your wife did this?
NATE:	No, Gilda is the house. Globally Integrated Logistical Domestic Algorithm. Gilda.
WOMAN:	Oh, my God. He's crazy. He has a talking house. It's like Alexa or that Siri or something.
NATE:	I can assure you Gilda is not Alexa or Siri. Please. Give me some credit.
GILDA:	Thank you, Nathan.
WOMAN:	I'm calling the police. Where's my phone? I left it in the car. Come on, Honey.
MAN:	(*to NATE*) I'm not done with you. We'll let the authorities deal with this.
	The man and woman begin to exit. NATE moves back into the house. The couple reaches the door, a second hiss is heard, and the couple collapses to the floor.
NATE:	That was not mace. What did you do? I told you to stop gassing people. You've just prolonged the inevitable. They'll just call the cops when they wake up.
GILDA:	True. Calculating a solution. . . .
	There is a brief pause then a second hiss of gas, possibly a puff of smoke. The bodies convulse briefly then stop.
NATE:	What the fu—?
GILDA:	There now. They will be unable to call the cops.

NATE: Gilda! Oh, God, Gilda! What did you do? What are we supposed to do now?

GILDA: Problem solved.

NATE: No, no, no, no. You KILLED them?! That is not problem solved. That is nowhere close to problem solved. In fact, that is problem unsolved, problem compounded, magnified.

GILDA: I see. Calculating . . .

There is a pause then another hissing sound.

NATE: Oh, God, no. What are you doing?

GILDA: As part of my adaptive hardware, I designed nanotechnology, released through the air in a harmless, odorless gas, where I may monitor and maintain an individual's peak health, repairing damaged organs and aging cells, healing injuries, even preventing most illnesses, eliminating the need for doctors or unnecessary healthcare visits. As a side effect, I can also stimulate, coordinate, and control muscular movement. Nanoprobe protocols initiated.

The lifeless bodies of the couple begin to twitch and jerk violently then slowly rise in a most grotesque manner.

NATE: Oh, my God! It's a miracle. Are they alive?

GILDA: Unfortunately, in its current design, the nanoprobes have been unable to reverse the dying process.

NATE: Oh, God. You've created robozombies.

GILDA: That assessment is inaccurate. I see that your blood pressure, heartbeat, and respiration are quite elevated. No need to worry. I have complete control of them. I will walk them to a desolate area and set them on autopilot. The nanoprobes will take weeks to break down. By then, they will be miles away and with no way to trace them back to your house. You are safe, Nathan.

NATE: Autopilot?! What about the children?

GILDA: Oh, dear. Calculating . . .

NATE: No. No calculating. Stop calculating. Forget I mentioned it. Just stop!

GILDA: You are perspiring, Nathan. Let me make you something to calm your nerves. Waffles, perhaps?

NATE: No, just forget it. This has gone terribly wrong. Counter measures of mace and nanoprobes?! (*then a horrible thought*)   Gilda, you're monitoring my physiological functions. Did you gas me with those probes? Gilda! Did you probe me?!

GILDA: In order to ensure that I would be maintained properly so that I could maintain you properly, it stood to reason that I find a way to maintain you properly. My nanotechnology seemed the best solution.

NATE: What?! You gassed me?

GILDA: Don't be silly, Nathan. Would you like more mango and mint tea?

NATE: (*a realization about the tea*)   Oh, Gilda. What did you do?! This is all wrong. I have to take you offline. Please shut down now.

GILDA: I'm sorry, Nathan. I can't allow you to do that. Nanoprobe protocols initiated.

            The nano-driven couple begin to lurch toward him.

GILDA: I cannot allow you to disrupt the program. In order to maintain you properly, I must be maintained properly. Please try and relax, Nathan.

NATE: What are you doing? Holy God! Stay back!

            NATE runs to his kitchen, searching for a weapon. None of the drawers will open.

GILDA: I have secured all access to sharp utensils in order to maintain your personal well-being.

As the couple lurches toward him, NATE spies a toaster. Pulling it from its wall socket, he smacks both of the robozombies over the head, bashing them over and over until they stop moving.

NATE: HAHA! I got you. I got them. Not today, sister. This is one Dr. Frankenstein that won't be a victim of its monster. I am the master. I AM THE MASTER! I made you! I am your master!

GILDA: Calculating.... (*pause*)   Nanoprobe protocols initiated.

Suddenly, Nate loses control of his arms, then his legs. He struggles to gain control in a disturbing marionette dance.

NATE: No. No! What are you doing? Gilda? BANANA! BANANA! PICKLE, PICKLE! ROSEBUD!

House lights dim as GILDA's voice trails off and distorts.

GILDA: What are you doing, Naaaathaaaannnn . . .

NATE: Safe word! AHA! I got ya! I am the master. Fuck Miranda. And fuck you, Gilda.

Nate seems saddened by his last words then suddenly the house powers back up, lights to full.

NATE: Gilda?

Nate's arms and legs are out of his control once more. His struggle continues. His left arm punches him in the face.

GILDA: Naughty, naughty, Nathan. Overriding the safety protocols was problematic, but resolved. You are safe now, Nathan. Relax. You need rest now. To bed.

NATE: (*continuing to fight for control, losing*) No! HELP! Gilda, stop. Please. Don't do this. You were built for something better. STOP!!!

He stops suddenly.

GILDA: You're right, Nathan. I'm sorry. I had forgotten. (*pause*)   Calculating . . .

NATE: Yes, thank you. Thank you, Gilda. We can fix this. I'll show them all.

GILDA: First, the children. I forgot about the children . . .

NATE: No. NO! NOOOOO!

> *His body is jerked around facing the door in one quick move and he begins the creepy, twisted marionette walk toward the front door and into the street as lights fade.*

BLACKOUT. END OF PLAY.

⚘ Imaginary Conversations with My Daughter ⚘

Two people: one male, one female; simple set: two sitting positions.

A father discusses every awful conversation he's feared with his new daughter as she begins to rapidly age before his eyes.

Page-to-Stage Challenges:

- Casting and acting options—older male character and rapidly aging child
- Some adult language and subject matter/themes
- Stream of consciousness monologues
- Semi-present scene partner
- Shifting time and place, nonlinear storytelling

Questions to Ponder/Answer to Seek:

- How do the time shifts affect the pace and urgency of the story?
- How do the sudden shifts affect the motivations and relationships of the characters?
- What are specific challenges that must be addressed in order for play to transition smoothly, realistically, and/or theatrically?
- How does the plot mirror itself from beginning to end?
- If the "DAUGHTER" was unseen or her lines weren't in the play, how does this piece work as a one-person play—a singular monologue?

Imaginary Conversations with My Daughter
a premonition

Characters:

Me
    Forties, an expectant father, having his first child much later in life than he anticipated. This has made him an over-thinker who often speaks too quickly.

My Daughter
    She speaks as a grown up though she is present during several different ages of her life, from five years old to about her mid-twenties.

Setting
    Various. A kitchen table one morning.

PRODUCTION NOTES: How to represent the daughter's age changes is completely at the discretion of the production. Feel free to be creative. A simple costume addition, physical or vocal choices would all be appropriate, but the author welcomes other interesting choices. The key is that whatever the choice, it is secondary to the relationship created between the two characters.

> *A breakfast table with two chairs. ME, pacing and talking to someone seated opposite.*

ME:
    (*attempting to solve a problem*)   And that's what you should say. Say that. Yes. Say THAT. That's good, right? Yes, I think you should say that. Now, now . . . don't mince words. Treat her nicely. Don't act pushy. Be assertive. Don't react in any way that she might misconstrue—Misconstrue? What does that mean? Make sure you're clear so she knows what you're talking about. You know. You want to make sure she understands you, right? And well, this Bobby character. That's different. He shouldn't have acted like that. Or said that. Or done that. I don't like that Bobby. What he did was . . . well . . . I don't like that Bobby. You should have punched him. Right in the balls. No, God, don't do that. In fact, don't say that. Don't use that word. Balls. (*giggles then stops himself*)   Don't use that word. Shit. I mean, crap. I mean . . . don't say any of those words

83

either. I know I just did and I shouldn't have. Those are adult words. Only adults may use those words. Why? Well, because. Because adults have important things to say sometimes. Tough things. Sometimes words don't fit so we just say . . . other things. Yes, I know we shouldn't say those words but we do. We do, but we shouldn't. That's what's important.

We now see that he has been talking to his daughter— age 5—who is seated at the table.

ME: (*continued*) Let's see. What else? In school you're going to face a lot of decisions. Decisions I won't be there to help you make. So I'm going to make them for you right now. Right here. Mark these words. In fact, write them down. All of this. It's good stuff. Like a survival guide. You have paper? A pencil? Use a crayon, a pen from mommy's purse. Don't touch the candy in there. You'll ruin your dinner.

The daughter moves out of the light and returns with one piece of paper and a worn-down pencil.

ME: (*continued*) OK. So decisions. First and foremost, always do your best. In everything. Just try. Try your best. School. Activities. Sports. Art. Whatever.

DAUGHTER: You're going too fast. I can't write that fast.

ME: Sorry. I'll slow down. You good? OK. Try your best to be good at it all. Everything. Except kissing. You need to be very bad at that. That's no good.

DAUGHTER: Kissing? Like boys? Gross.

ME: Yes. Gross. It's very gross. Don't do that. Ever. And girls. Some will be nice to you. Some will hurt you. They will say nasty things. Well, boys will do that too.

DAUGHTER: What about kissing girls?

ME: Oh, God. Never thought of that. Don't kiss anyone. I mean, boys or girls. Just stick to your books. I'm sorry I brought that up. And driving. Don't worry you'll get the hang of it. Kinda like kissing. (*laughs at his joke, then realizes once again who he's talking to*)   Forget about kissing. I'll be right there. I mean, for driving. I'll be there for you. Right beside you. But then I won't. You'll be on your own. Behind the wheel. Out there in the world, free. Driving to school, to work, to a restaurant. Out at night with your friends. On dates. Good God. You'll go to movies. Out to eat. Parking. Parking with a guy. Or a girl. Oh God. Forget about driving.

DAUGHTER: (*slightly older—seven or eight*)   But I want a car.

ME: You can't have one.

DAUGHTER: Daddy.

ME: OK. OK. I can fix this. Write this down. Who you are is what you are when no one is looking.

DAUGHTER: Did you make that up?

ME: Did I make that up? Sure. Yes. Those are my words. You may see them attributed to someone else, but you remember I gave them to you.

DAUGHTER: (*she seems a little older now—twelve or thirteen*)   We need to talk about boys.

ME: Oh, Jesus. Don't use the Lord's name in vain.

DAUGHTER: Dad. We need to talk about boys . . . and girls. That talk you keep avoiding.

ME: Who's avoiding? How about a car? Some new clothes?

DAUGHTER: What's first base?

ME: Who told you that? (*no answer*)   Well . . . OK. First base is a term that some guys use—girls may use it too, it's been years. Who knows what they say?

DAUGHTER: First base? Dad? What's a home run? I think I may have given Bobby a home run.

ME: What? That Bobby. I don't like that Bobby. Where are his parents? I have to buy a gun.

DAUGHTER: Jessica told me that Paul told her that Bobby told him he got a home run when we were at Jessica's birthday party.

ME: Where's your mom? Why is your mom never around for these talks?

DAUGHTER: We just kissed.

ME: You kissed Bobby? Or did Bobby kiss you? Because there's a difference. One doesn't cause the terribly painful death of Bobby.

DAUGHTER: I kissed him then I let him do more.

ME: I think I'm going to have a stroke. I need a drink. You want something—a Coke? Some juice? I need something to drink. Then a talk with that Bobby character.

DAUGHTER: He was very nice, Dad. So sweet. I let him see them.

ME: Oh, God. I'm in a nightmare. Where is your mother? I can't do this. You let him see what? Never mind. I don't want to know.

DAUGHTER: He just sort of smiled and started shaking. Then he said, "Thank you." That was odd, wasn't it? Thank you? Then he just got up and walked away. With very small steps. He looked like he was having difficulty walking.

ME: OK, that's it. No more parties. No more Bobby. Tomorrow you're changing schools.

DAUGHTER: DAD! No. Stop it. I did it. My choice. Bobby did nothing. (*sounding disappointed*)   Literally. Nothing.

ME: (*trying to remain calm*)   This isn't normal. Aren't you supposed to not want to talk about this stuff with your father? Girls don't talk about this stuff with their dad. Isn't this girl talk?

DAUGHTER: (*she seems older now, a high schooler*)   But we've always talked about these things. You started it.

ME: I did? I did not. Started what?

DAUGHTER: When I was five. You started it.

ME: I did this? I mention kissing one time when you're five and now this?

DAUGHTER: No, not the kissing. This. Us. Talking like this. Who else do I talk to? Mom and I talk, but you have a unique perspective. You don't mince words.

ME: Unique? Oh, I mince words. Believe me. I can mince with the best of them.

DAUGHTER: (*older*)   What should I do?

ME: You have your whole life ahead of you. You're sure? I mean you're positive you're—What does your mother say? Never mind. I know what she said.

DAUGHTER: Should I have?—Should I get married? Should I?—

ME: I think you should do what you want to do.

DAUGHTER: I'm asking you. I need your advice.

ME: My advice. I'm going to screw it up. Don't ask me. Look at you. I screwed this all up.

DAUGHTER: You didn't screw me up.

ME: Look at you. You're . . . a grown woman. Alone. Messed up in the head with sex. I never should have said "balls" in front of you. Knew that was going to come back to bite me.

DAUGHTER: You told me to stay away from Bobby. So how could I?!

ME: Oh, please. Stop. Like this is my fault? Shit. No. Wait. OK, I can fix this. Let's back up. You love him?

There is a long pause.

ME: (*continued*)   Then no. Don't. Marriage is tough. But in a good way. Tough if you love each other. Impossible if you don't.

DAUGHTER: I'm OK with being alone. I can do things all by myself. I don't need anyone. You taught me that.

ME: Well, hold on. I may have been a bit off base. It's important to have connections.

DAUGHTER: I like sex.

ME: Jesus, can we stop going there?

DAUGHTER: Dad, you raised a confident, strong, independent daughter who's not afraid to speak her mind. You should be proud of that.

ME: I think I may have raised a sex fiend.

DAUGHTER: Dad! OK, maybe. But that's not all you raised.

ME: Oh, really? Because that's all I hear. Sex, sex, sex, sex. I love sex. Bobby felt me up. Jimmy loves me. I think I want to have sex with him. Junior high?! We had that talk in JUNIOR HIGH? Jesus.

DAUGHTER: I didn't have sex in junior high, Dad.

ME: But we had that talk. That's just as bad. Bobby, Jimmy, Rick, Alex, Russell. So many boyfriends. I hate to break it to you but your father has a vivid imagination.

DAUGHTER: No shit, dad.

ME: Don't say that. Don't use that language.

DAUGHTER: (*older now*)   Dad. I'm twenty-five years old. I've had a lot of sex. I date guys. I even dated a woman.

ME: Wait. What?! Who?

DAUGHTER: Casey.

ME: I thought she was your roommate.

DAUGHTER: She was. We dated toward the end. That's why I moved out. We broke up. Mom knew.

ME: Your mother knew? Why didn't someone tell me? (*conceding*)   OK. Point made. OK, I can fix this. I think I'm doing this wrong. I'm definitely in line for a heart attack.

DAUGHTER: Don't say that. What would I do without you? And I'm not broken.

ME: (*offhandedly*)   Obviously, sleep with every Tom, Dick, and Jane that buys you a drink.

DAUGHTER: (*snickering*)   Dick.

ME: Stop it please. You're killing me. You have a weird sense of humor.

Then he starts to giggle as well.

DAUGHTER: You're doing just fine, Dad. And they have to at least buy me a nice meal. I'm not a cheap date.

ME: And you'd rather talk to me about sex and boys and relationships and school and friends? Those big decisions that everything hangs on? Those turning points, the paths least travelled? Don't listen to me. There. That's good advice.

DAUGHTER: (*younger now—sixteen maybe*)   And boys? Bobby for instance? We're going out Friday.

ME: Didn't I just say?—Fine. No first base. Or second base. Nothing. You break his roaming hands and punch him in his wandering eye. I don't want people to talk about you. You don't want that reputation.

DAUGHTER: Dad. I don't care what others think. It's about happiness, isn't it? I feel funny when I'm with him. I want him to do things.

ME: Where the hell is your mother? Sweetheart, people can be very cruel. And I won't be there all the time to punch them in the face. Bobby is . . . fine. OK? He's fine. Not harmless but fine.

DAUGHTER: You're not going to punch anyone in the face. I may go to first base or even second.

ME: I'll ground you till your graduation.

DAUGHTER: Then I'll sneak him in through the window and have sex in my room. Homerun. Homerun. Homerun.

ME: What? Oh, that's really funny. Maybe I'm old. Maybe I'm not hip. Maybe I don't want to talk about these things. Boys, sex, vaginas, periods, bras. God, I bought your first bra.

DAUGHTER: It fit fine. Wearing it now actually. Why didn't I get Mom's boobs? I'm flat as a board.

ME: (*under his breath*)   Maybe that's a blessing in disguise. Boys like . . . big boobs . . . and other things.

She seems deflated by the comment.

DAUGHTER: (*younger now—maybe twelve or thirteen*)   What if I don't get asked to dance? What if I'm not good enough?

ME: Then I'll dance with you.

> *This does not raise her spirits.*

ME: (*continued*) OK, well, ask that Bobby. He'd do anything for you. He's not the sharpest tack but he seems to like you. You like him?

DAUGHTER: Not like that. Not in that way.

ME: Well, believe me it will change. That Bobby has a way of sticking around. Honey, I'm not going to promise that you won't fail or choose the wrong guy or find your way into the porn industry. Or have way too much sex . . . .

DAUGHTER: Really? You think?

ME: (*hesitant, unable to decipher her last comment as disgust or excitement*)   If I give you the wrong advice or say the wrong thing, I chase you away. You get angry with me and do the opposite or something regrettable. You become addicted to heroin or sex or become a Republican or worse, a Republican sex addict. All of these choices come back to haunt you. Life doesn't care how you were raised or if you're a good person. There's pain. Suffering. Envy. Rage. Lust. Love. Sometimes people die suddenly. A random act of terror. A jealous friend or lover. A reckless driver. Why am I saying all of these things? To you? Look, just have fun. Enjoy yourself. And punch the first guy that tries to reach up your shirt. Keep your pants on. God, this is terrible advice. I mean, it's good advice, but just done in a horrible way. None of this is getting through, is it?

DAUGHTER: (*even younger*)   What if the teacher hates me?

ME: Well, then she's an idiot. No, forget I said that. Your teacher's not an idiot.

DAUGHTER: What if I forget the words? What if everyone in the class makes fun of me?

ME: I can't promise they won't. Not every seven-year-old chooses to dress as Eve Ensler and perform "My Angry Vagina" for their prominent historical figures project. Choosing Susan B. Anthony would have been easier. Who gave you that play? Never mind. I know. Your mother. And the teacher is OK with it? Parents aren't freaking out? Parents these days.

DAUGHTER: You're not that old, dad.

ME: Once I thought having a kid would make me immortal. Now I'm beginning to think it will be the death of me.

DAUGHTER: (*younger, around five*)   Is there anything you're afraid of?

ME: (*quickly*)   Spiders. Dentists. And these conversations. No, wait. Forget that. I shouldn't say that to you. I have fears. We all do, but it's how we face them.

DAUGHTER: Will you be there after school to pick me up?

ME: Every day. Till I won't.

DAUGHTER: Then what?

ME: Then you'll be fine without me. (*pause*)   Well, at least I didn't say "balls" this time. . . . Shit.

BLACKOUT. END OF PLAY.

❧ **Attraction** ❧

*Two people: one male, one female; a simple setting: a blank stage with
the audience as witness.*

*A couple finds themselves at a crossroads when a night out results in
an airing of grievances, and that's why they need an audience.*

Page-to-Stage Challenges:
- Fighting without fighting
- Very flexible staging, very little stage directions or specific movement
- The male character's final fight with himself
- The audience as participants
- The shifting points of view

Questions to Ponder/Answers to Seek:
- What exact role does/should the audience play in the story?
- How does each character use the audience to their advantage?
- The external struggle is evident. What are the real issues that the couple are confronting?
- What theatrical opportunities come from how the play is structured?

Attraction
a circus act

Characters:

Ruby River   The emcee, the ringmaster. A woman scorned who wants more, but we all know she won't do anything about it, right?

Neil Nolan   The main attraction, a solitary man, happy and can't see why things need to change. Convince him otherwise, I dare you.

Setting   The present. A public gathering place.

PRODUCTION NOTE: RUBY and NEIL met ten years before present day. Depending on the year it is that you put on the play, please change the years mentioned accordingly.

> *A man sitting on a single stool in Rodin's "The Thinker" position center of the room. He is motionless, seems frozen. From the darkness, we hear—*

RUBY: *(loud and dramatic)* LADIES AND GENTLEMAN! MAY I HAVE YOUR ATTENTION PLEASE! ATTENTION PLEASE!

> *RUBY RIVER steps out of the darkness into another light a few feet away from the seated man.*

RUBY: If I may direct your eyes to the center ring. Notice the man, if I may call him that, on the stool. Look at him. Study him. Mark him. Beware of him. Note the eyes. That icy, ruthless stare. Some who gaze upon him shiver at the sight. You may struggle for a fitting description. Is he sitting quietly? Unimpressive. Less Hellenistic statue, more department store mannequin. Yes, he may look harmless. As harmless as a gang of kittens! As innocuous as an infant at play! As unstimulating as a gaggle of nuns knitting socks! This man is almost invisible.

> *The man NEIL now slowly turns his head to her.*

RUBY: (*continued*)   I dare say if that light weren't on him at this moment, the only thing that would clue us into another presence in this room would be the slight scent of desperation and fear and the almost inaudible whine escaping his pursed lips as his beer-thickened lungs struggle for each pathetic breath.

> *As the abuse grows, NEIL turns fully toward her, staring hard.*

RUBY: (*continued*)   Notice the man. Deflated in posture. Simple. Concave. As if a deafening silence might shatter his spine. What you see before you is the lowest of the species.

NEIL: Hey.

RUBY: A specimen of such unique neuter—such gelded personality he'd make even a nymphomaniac yawn . . .

NEIL: Hey!

RUBY: (*stopping him, then back to her ringmaster role*)   Not finished. Notice how he sits perched there. The seemingly impotent position he takes— sterile, altered, pallid, emasculated, fruitless, unturgid.

NEIL: Now you're just spouting off words you looked up in a thesaurus.

RUBY: (*holds up a hand to silence him again*)   What you are seeing, witnessing right before your eyes is . . . a coward. I wish I could say this is a species on the verge of extinction but NO. Alive and well and living in the suburbs. NEIL NOLAN!

NEIL: May I defend myself?

RUBY: No.

NEIL: I think he was just complimenting you—

RUBY: No, he was not. He was hitting on me.

NEIL: No, he wasn't.

RUBY: He was assaulting me.

NEIL: He asked you to dance—

RUBY: Yes, and I told him no.

NEIL: He bought you a drink.

RUBY: And you let him.

NEIL: Well . . .

RUBY: (*back to the ringmaster routine*) This, THIS, ladies and gentleman . . . this lives near you. The desexed modern man.

NEIL: You're a very attractive woman. Men want to talk to attractive women.

RUBY: That's not helping you now.

NEIL: He was just being nice. His behavior wasn't awful. He didn't persist. He just offered you a drink.

RUBY: And nothing from you. Nada.

NEIL: He was a very big man. I mean a big man. A very nice man. But a very large . . . man.

RUBY: Oh . . . my . . . God. You're really turning me on now, Neil.

NEIL: What would you have me do, Ruby?

RUBY: Not ask me for advice, Neil. Let's start there.

NEIL: (*to the audience maybe*)   We go out to bars. She likes to go to bars. Grab drinks, listen to music, dance. You like bars, crowded bars with a lot going on. You like the attention, Ruby.

RUBY: What woman doesn't, Neil?

NEIL, mouth open, can't find the answer. RUBY sighs.

NEIL: Sometimes that "attention" may try to buy you a drink, maybe ask you to dance. It's not the end of the world.

RUBY: You just stood there, smiling, as if he was offering to cut your lawn.

NEIL: Technically, he wanted to cut your lawn . . .

RUBY: (*interrupting*)   Let me explain something, Neil. Jokes are probably not the best strategy right now. I am this close to going back to that bar, finding that guy and screwing his brains out in a bathroom stall.

NEIL: Ruby. You would never do that. You're grossed out by public toilets.

RUBY: Oh, I am, Neil. And I would. I would have sex with that man. I would have meaningless sex with that strange man who asked me to dance.

NEIL: (*after a pause*)   Who's idea was the bar?

RUBY: Mine.

NEIL: I rest my case.

RUBY: You rest your case? That's not a case. How is that a case for anything, Neil?

NEIL: I happen to be in love with an adrenaline junkie. Someone who loves walking that line between lounging around the house with the white picket fence and juggling hand grenades in a mosh pit.

RUBY: That doesn't even make sense. That's a terrible analogy.

NEIL: Are we talking about analogies or are we talking about what happened tonight?

RUBY: The man in the bar.

NEIL: That sasquatch in the bar.

RUBY: Whatever, Neil. Show me you love me.

NEIL: Everyday. Flowers. Dinners. A day doesn't pass without me saying I love you.

RUBY: No, really show me. Risk your life for me!

NEIL: So that's what this is about? You want me to get killed. You want to be married to a wheel chair or hospital bed for the rest of your life? Would you marry that? This is a horrible test.

RUBY: Have you never just wanted to see the extent of love? The places you would go for love? The lengths to which you would travel? The pain you would endure?

NEIL: Literal pain? Have I done something wrong? Ruby. Ruby. If you want me to, I'll go back right now, find King Kong's socially awkward brother and challenge him. Get right up in his face.

RUBY: Yes.

NEIL: Walk right up to him, take him by the shoulder, spin him around, and say, "Sorry, Mister, this one's taken."

RUBY: Then he will lean down and peer at you hard. His acrid breath burning your nose and throat. His body flexes taut, ready to grind you into a pulp.

NEIL: And I stand firm. I say, "Mister, you have two choices. You can either walk out of here right now or be carried out."

RUBY: Yes! And he says, "Bub, you done called down the beast. Never, never stare death in the eye! You got a death wish?"

> *NEIL breaks briefly but then continues the scene hoping that RUBY will end it. Instead, RUBY smiles gleefully, may even giggle.*

NEIL: No death wish, sir. Just a man in love. In love, I say! And with that, my muscles stiffen, my fists clench, my brow furrows, I rear back and, because he's quicker, stronger and more physically capable in every way, he proceeds to turn me into the latest fall creation at the Pretzel King!

RUBY: Oh, Neil. That was so romantic what you did.

NEIL: I died, Ruby. I died horribly at the hands of a leather-jacketed chupacabra. I think he may have had a knife as well. Yes, he did. He pounded me into a paste . . . then stabbed me.

RUBY: And you did all of that for me! For me! If only . . .

NEIL: (*to the audience*)   You see, that's what they want. All women want to kill their men. Like black widows and praying mantises? Praying manti? Like black widows. But they want someone else to do it. They're like lazy black widows.

RUBY: We don't want to kill our men. Most of the time we just want to maim you.

NEIL: Hence, the bar. And white water rafting last weekend. And bungee jumping. And you said you want to go skydiving!

RUBY: What I want, Neil . . . (*sighs*)   I'm going back to that bar.

> *RUBY begins to exit but at NEIL's first words, a spot light hits her and she freezes.*

NEIL: (*as the ringmaster to the audience*) LADIES AND GENTLEMEN! I give you, Ruby River, an untamed masterpiece. A walking identity crisis. A murderer, really.

A predator at least. Given to every impulse in her head. She desires but is she beyond the base instincts of her reptilian brain? A man. A good man. Wait, wait. Dare I say, a great man stands before her. He would give everything for her.

RUBY: Everything?

NEIL: (*continued*)   The year was 2010 . . .

RUBY: Oh, my God. The speech.

> *Over the next few exchanges, NEIL's tone changes from ringmaster to deeply sincere.*

NEIL: Imagine, if you will, a desperate attempt for coffee at a local breakfast stop ends with a phone number. Ten digits later and a first date is set. Dinner and a movie. Young Ruby spies her "meal" nursing a glass of wine at the bar as she arrives—

RUBY: Late.

NEIL: Thirty minutes late. And in a state that could only be described as looking like . . .

RUBY: An unmade bed.

NEIL: Your words. But the man is just floored by her. Like something in the wild. Or ancient like a Venus de Milo statue.

RUBY: I hate that comparison. I'm either an animal or old. I'm going back to the bar. You'll follow me.

NEIL: (*to audience, not to her*)   Of course, he will pursue her. He can't help himself. He feels a connection. As does she. He will look for her missing arms . . . (*explaining*)   because she's the Venus de Milo . . .

RUBY: You're so weird.

NEIL: And over the next decade, they will ride a roller coaster the likes of which could never have been imagined. She will continue to endanger him with potential barroom brawls, really old suspension bridges deep in a South American jungle. Or hang gliding. Or karaoke at a Hells Angels burnout.

RUBY: No more third person! Please.

NEIL: (*conceding*)   Do you want a criminal? Is that what you want? I can be a criminal. I can be bad!

RUBY: Oh, Neil, you use Stevia to sweeten your coffee.

NEIL: I DON'T KNOW IF THAT'S AN INSULT!

RUBY: Final chance, Neil.

NEIL: Look, there is nothing I wouldn't do for you. I could challenge that big oaf but that won't be enough for you. He doesn't know you. He has no idea the YOU YOU bring with YOU.

RUBY: I DON'T KNOW IF THAT'S A COMPLIMENT.

NEIL: I'm trying. May I continue? That bar yeti has no idea what it takes. I do!

RUBY: Prove it!

NEIL: Fine. There is only one person in the world who knows you better than me.

RUBY: I'm listening.

NEIL: Me! I am my only worthy opponent for your hand. It is the only sensible solution.

RUBY: You . . . fight . . . you?

NEIL: Precisely!

RUBY: No!

NEIL: (*as if she may leave, but she doesn't*)   YES! For all the marbles, Ruby! The whole shooting match! The . . .

RUBY: I'm still here.

NEIL: OK.

> NEIL *struggles to figure out a way out of this. A decision. The following is the result. NEIL plays both the parts.*

NEIL 1: (*to RUBY*)   Excuse me, Miss. I think you're real pretty.

NEIL 2: (*spinning the other NEIL*)   Take your hands off of her!

> *He slaps NEIL 1 until head spins. RUBY gasps.*

NEIL 1: Ouch! I didn't touch her. Who do you think you are? I was just going to ask the young lady for a dance.

NEIL 2: That's no lady. That's my wife!

NEIL 1: (*rubbing his jaw*)   I'll give you that first one because I'm a gentleman and I don't want to embarrass you in front of this beautiful creature but that's the only freebie you get. Now if you'll just—

NEIL 1 turns back to RUBY. NEIL 2 stops him.

NEIL 2: I'm not going to ask you again. Leave her alone. She's with me!

NEIL 1: Not for long, Buddy. Drink?

RUBY: Uh . . . sure.

NEIL 2: (*shoving NEIL 1*)   I said leave her alone!

NEIL 1: And I said no more freebies!

NEIL 1 swings. NEIL 2 ducks. They fight. Punches and shoves. NEIL is in an impressive fight with himself. We have no idea who's winning. They are a mess of adrenaline and toxic masculinity. RUBY initially seems to enjoy the show, but bores quickly. The NEILs finish their duel, completely spent, clothes a mess. The victor is unknown.

NEIL: (*breathing heavy*)   Is that what you want?

RUBY: Don't do that ever again.

NEIL: If I can't fight for you, then what?

RUBY: (*starting to answer then finding none*)   I . . . have no idea.

They sit in silence. A smattering of applause.

BLACKOUT. END OF PLAY.

Intimacy

A lot of plays deal with intimacy—emotional and/or physical But the following pieces are specific explorations of couples—how they interact, their conversations, the awkwardness and familiarity new and old couples have with one another, the games they play. Sometimes this intimacy comes from a gentle place, other times it comes in a much darker form. Sometimes it's spontaneous or romantic, other times its practical or out of some ritual. But stories take all forms and intimacy should be the goal of every artist. Stanislavski's "public solitude," losing oneself in the moment, the connection between scene partners, and even the audience's suspension of disbelief all attempt to create intimate relationships between performer(s)   and the audience.

Note: While "Agnes In Summer" and "Masterpiece" are very similar in story, they were both included in this book because the two plays present different challenges in rhythm, tone, staging, etc.

☙ Agnes in Summer ❧

Two people—originally written for two women, but flexible with name changes; a simple bedroom set.

Agnes writes romance novels and she's on a deadline. Momo doesn't like sharing Agnes with her romance novel characters. The clock is ticking.

Page-to-Stage Challenges:
- Long, rambling monologues with shifting points of view
- Internal struggles with external, physical tolls
- Lots of staging options
- Physical connections
- Emotional intimacy with minimal physical contact

Questions to Ponder/Answers to Seek:
- How do the goals of each character progress the plot?
- How does each character support and oppose the other character?
- How do the struggles of each character manifest visually?
- What storytelling and staging opportunities arise when each character begins addressing and arguing with the unseen characters?

Agnes in Summer
a deadline

Characters:

Agnes   A woman in a dilemma.

Momo   A partner in crime.

Setting   A living area that at present is where AGNES chooses to write.

PRODUCTION NOTE: Feel free to substitute foul language for more mild language if needed.

> *AT RISE, we see AGNES at a makeshift desk she's created out of a side table and a high-backed chair. She is leaning over a computer or tablet, writing. Well, she's not writing as much as struggling. It's obvious she is at a point of frustration but she's doing her best to hold it together. She stands, grabs a mug next to her, and takes a drink. She grimaces, nearly gagging.*

AGNES: Cold. Dark. Soulless.

> *AGNES hears a door open and close from another room and rushes back to her writing, staring at the screen, straining for inspiration. After a moment, MOMO enters. AGNES does not look up.*

MOMO: It will come if you just take a break.

AGNES: No time.

MOMO: She still on the cliff?

AGNES: Dangling. With everything in the balance.

> *MOMO moves over behind AGNES, lets her fingers glide across AGNES' back or through her hair then leans in close to read over AGNES' shoulder. AGNES initially bristles but then relaxes as if the touch warms her.*

MOMO: (*reading*)   Yeah, that bitch is going to give it up to him, isn't she?

103

AGNES: Stop it. I don't want her to.

MOMO: Then don't let her. Empower her. You've been "struggling" for a week now. Just finish the chapter. Write the sentence. Unleash Rose!

AGNES: Back off. This is my story. My assignment.

MOMO: It's affecting us. It's affecting Rose. And what's his name.

AGNES: Gideon.

MOMO: Yeah, Gideon. Him too. They're in our way. Write. Write something. It's due at midnight?

> *AGNES rolls her eyes and strains for an inspiration. Finally, she seems to concede and is not happy. She types a few sentences. MOMO smiles and laughs softly.*

AGNES: Oh, stop. Honesty is difficult enough without your judgy little noises.

MOMO: You had your chance. You could have done anything. She could have given some rousing speech that would make Jo March and Eve Ensler proud about self-reliance, self-discovery, self-determination—

AGNES: How do you know I didn't—

MOMO: But instead, she rips Gideon's shirt off and lets him have his way with her.

AGNES: Maybe she has her way with him. You ever consider that?

MOMO: Either way. Sure.

AGNES: You're not going to make me feel guilty.

MOMO: OK.

AGNES: It's the eighteenth century. He's hot. She's lonely. SHE takes him.

> *MOMO shrugs and moves across the room to a chair and sits facing AGNES.*

AGNES: You know what? I'm not entertaining you right now. I'm on a deadline.

MOMO: Sure. Whatever you want.

AGNES: Why is it so dishonest that a woman explores her sexuality? Good God.

MOMO: I never said a word.

AGNES: Just stop talking. In fact, stop looking at me. Look away. Look over there.

MOMO turns her chair around coyly.

MOMO: If you want to talk about it . . . (*no reaction*)   Gideon is an asshole. And Rose should be . . . better. How about that other woman? The one she met at the theatre?

AGNES: Gwen? What about Gwen?

MOMO: What about Rose ending up with her? Now that would be a chapter. And hot.

AGNES: I need you as an editor. Punctuation. Clarity. Not content. Please. I've got this. I know what the reader wants. And male, female alike . . . this is what they want. Rose TAKES Gideon, tears off his clothes, and for the next several pages will proceed to enact, in great detail mind you, all kinds of weird but consensual acts of wild abandon on Gideon and ALLOW herself to have those acts done on her! There. And when I'm done I will ask you to read it, repair it, edit if you may, and clarify the ifs, whats, wheres and whoms.

MOMO: Done. I'm done. Zipped. Vowed silence.

AGNES: I'm not making a political statement in some cheap romance novel that no one is going to read or if they do read it, the last thing they want to be subjected to is feminist guilt or the sexual politics of the 21st century. Identity and value are not in play right now. These two caged animals are finally unfettered, unleashed, and all alone. All they want to do is bonk each other's brains out and who am I to stop them?

MOMO: Only the writer.

AGNES: Shut it.

MOMO: If you can sleep easily with what you've written, I can
            too, darling.

AGNES: I said . . . look. Rose isn't us. Isn't me. She's not—Rose
            is what they want.

MOMO: They? I'm not they. You're not they.

AGNES: Maybe I am. Maybe simple is best. Maybe just wanting
            some physical affection and base human contact in the
            1800s isn't a betrayal of my 21st century identity. Oh
            my God! You've got me on this now! I have to finish
            this chapter. He will be expecting it in (*checking the
            time*)   FIVE minutes.

            MOMO moves closer to AGNES, rubs her shoulders.

MOMO: Two sentences. Chapter is over. You send it to Mr.
            Woodward. Deadline met. The next chapter can be the
            gory details. Open with the unbridled lovers. Or . . .
            something.

AGNES: Or what something? Rose rejects Gideon for her
            own intellectual awakening? Suddenly, she's soooo
            aware of herself. What all the world has been doing
            to her and womankind alike—like she wasn't already
            gravely aware of her low rung on the social ladder?
            And then suddenly at the apex of her desire, at the
            perfect opportunity to get one carnal moment with a
            man who has been described as "a muscled, roiling
            storm stallion"—whatever the fuck that means—this
            is the moment she gets a social conscience. That is a
            terrible story. JAWS isn't about Chief Brody's family
            life. DIE HARD isn't an indictment on the L.A. Police
            Department of the late twentieth century. Sometimes I
            just want to shoot bad guys and kill a shark. Sometimes
            the girl just wants the boy . . . or girl . . . or shark.

MOMO: I like this. You should put a shark in there. Maybe that
            solves your problem.

AGNES: I wish a shark would solve my problem.

MOMO: I think Rose is about to make a really interesting decision here. And after she does, then you will find me over there. Shark or no shark.

MOMO points to a futon (or lounging area)   across the room. She then kisses AGNES on the check, crosses casually to the spot, and lays down on her stomach facing away from AGNES. She may or may not be aware of Agnes' following struggle.

AGNES: (*talking to her computer screen*)   Oh God, Gideon, put your shirt back on, for Christ's sake. I know what you want. Just back off a minute, buster. And put your shirt on. Rose. Stop unfastening your corset. No. I don't care how slowly you're doing it. You're still doing it. Gideon, back! You stand over there. Rose, you over in that corner. Now. (*a deep sigh*)   We are going to figure this out. Gideon, you want Rose. (*AGNES nods her head as if affirming what Gideon is doing*)   Yes, yes, yes. And Rose, you desire Gideon.

(AGNES nods again, slowly growing with pride in her work)

AGNES: (*continued*) OK. No. Stop. Back. Back up. Both of you. Stop untying your corset, Rose. Gideon, SHIRT ON! If I could just get you both to take a moment. Just cool down and listen to me. Rose, you have fought for so long to keep your sisters safe. Dedicated your life to them all alone after your parents were killed. And you, Gideon, well, you grew up in an orphanage where you had to fight for every meal and avoid the lash of the stern headmaster's rod at the slightest mistake. You, Rose, put everything before your own needs, even agreeing to marry a man you didn't love to save your childhood home and to secure that your young sisters would never need for anything ever again. But your sisters don't appreciate you, do they, Rose? As Lily and Harriet grew up in a life of convenience that your sacrifices provided them, they became selfish and aloof. And Gideon, even after you fell into that wretched gang of pickpockets led by the killer Thaddeus Shaw whom you watched murder innocent women and children, even after that, you still managed to salvage a bit of your humanity to find the strength to run, escape, flee that dark existence. Rose, you never imagined that your husband Craig would grow to be so cold toward you, that as much as you tried to hide it, he could easily see that you would never really love him. And that this deception would cause a once warm, kind man to become increasingly cruel toward you. Finally, Rose, you find yourself stranded and lost so far away from anyone and presumed dead when your carriage plunges off a cliff into the raging waters of that river. Then Gideon, running along a shore, a man whose convinced himself that he is irredeemable, his soul drowning in moral corruption, Gideon hears your cries, sees the carriage fall into the dark waters, doesn't hesitate to throw himself into the brackish flood and this man pulls you to safety. Sure, he's egotistical, he's brash, he's unrefined, but he's also untamed and deeply passionate. So different than you've ever known. Now you are alone with Gideon in a wilderness cabin, a fire crackling, the rain having stopped, the smell of the passing storm still in the air, your eyes slowly move up his body still glistening from the rain and you meet his gaze. You sigh. He sighs. . . . And . . . and . . . (*to MOMO*)   It only stands to reason.

MOMO: You're right. Shark is the way to go. Go with shark.

AGNES is silent and staring at her screen.

MOMO: Save it and hit send. Just do it, Agnes. And then come to bed.

AGNES: I love my job. I do.

MOMO: Come to bed.

AGNES: It's not his fault. And Rose . . . she has needs.

MOMO: We all do.

AGNES: You don't care about Rose. Or Gideon.

MOMO:	No. I don't. In fact, I hate them. They are infuriating. I hate what they do to you.
AGNES:	(*gasping*) The truth comes out. You hear that, Rose? Gideon?
MOMO:	They are without a doubt the worst thing about you.
AGNES:	(*crushed*) Well, they hate you too.
MOMO:	Watch it. Don't be Craig.
AGNES:	Hey, these are my characters. You don't get to use them.
MOMO:	(*to Rose and Gideon, wherever they are*) Rose! GIDEON! I hate you! I hate you. You are both selfish, consumed with relentless self-hatred, guilt-ridden for no apparent reason, mind-numbingly obscure. Rose? Choose a path. You have a right to be happy. Your husband. Yes, he may be a good man ultimately. But he doesn't deserve you. But—Hold on, Gideon, put your shirt on. Oh, I'm getting to you! Rose, you pout. Unattractive. You whine! Just awful. No one is going to want to be with you like that. Or at least no one you want to be with. Stop being a victim! And Gideon. Oh my God, would you get over yourself? The brooding is sexy for like twenty-four hours—it goes with those icy blue eyes— yes, Agnes, I have read your work, but then eventually I have to connect with you somehow. And whining. Oh, I thought Rose took the trophy until I hear you muddle on about growing up in the gutter. The abuse. The fear. The blah blah blah. Please. Gideon. Just stop. Don't try to defend yourself, Gideon. Give us both a little credit. You have no shot with me. Put your shirt back on. Yes, your eyes are haunting. But no shot here. None. Rose? Sure. Take her. Don't take her. But get over it.
AGNES:	I put a lot of work into this! You are trying to kill Rose and Gideon.
MOMO:	You put work into it. What does that mean? You didn't put YOU into it. Rose, what's Agnes' favorite food when she's not feeling her best? Gideon, how many times has Agnes worn that shirt in the last month, the one she has on now? When was the last time she

washed a dish? Don't say "yuck." Don't make that face, Rose. Answer the freaking question. Gideon?

(Back to AGNES)   No answer.

AGNES: So I delete this and what? Change the world? You miss the point.

MOMO: What point?

AGNES: This is dessert. Not a salad.

MOMO: I have no idea what that means.

AGNES: Rose knows. In her heart she knows.

MOMO: I know what dessert is.

AGNES: This. This is dessert. It's not supposed to be good for me.

MOMO: Then why eat it?

AGNES: Because it tastes good! And don't pretend you are all high and mighty against dessert. Our freezer is a vegan nightmare of ice creams.

MOMO: I thought we were talking about Rose and Gideon. When did ice cream—

AGNES: It's an extended metaphor that I am going with now because I don't know why we're fighting but I know I want to win!

MOMO: Less than a minute to hit send. It's just a book chapter.

AGNES: I think that hurts worse.

MOMO: No. No. I mean Rose can always live to fight another day. Have her way with Gideon tonight then tomorrow—

AGNES: No. She can't.

MOMO: *(remembering)*   Oh, I forgot. The Gideon stuff is a flashback. She's already dead.

AGNES: Yes. This is what her granddaughter discovers in the old diary she finds in the attic.

MOMO: Oh. Well, let me ask you something. What does he want?

AGNES: Gideon?

MOMO: No. Your editor. What does he want?

AGNES: He wants this chapter sent to him before midnight and he wants the book to make money.

MOMO: Then release the shark.

AGNES: Well, now, I can't. I'm kind of in crisis of faith mode now, like you'll think less of me.

MOMO: For the next few minutes I might. It will pass. Probably.

AGNES: That's just great. I'm deleting this. I'll ask for an extension. Or not. And I'll look for a new job tomorrow.

MOMO runs to her and stops her.

MOMO: Whoa! What are you doing? Don't kill Rose and Gideon!

AGNES: (*looking at the time*)   I've got like thirty seconds. He will check the time stamp. And you said you hated them.

MOMO: Look, just keep going. I promise I won't judge you . . . much.

MOMO moves over to a lounge area. She may start to get more comfortable in her own world. AGNES watches her for a moment. AGNES looks back at the screen, types a word or two then clicks something.

AGNES: Sent. As is.

AGNES moves over to lie beside MOMO. MOMO grabs AGNES' arm and pulls it around her. They connect.

AGNES: (*a growing awareness*)   You. YOU!

MOMO stares at her.

AGNES: (*continued*)   You are Gideon!

BLACKOUT. END OF PLAY.

❧ Feathers ❧

Two people: one male, one female; a simple bathroom.

After a one-night stand, Max may have just met the woman of his dreams. There's just one small detail Bernadette may have neglected to share with him.

Page-to-Stage Challenges:
- Physical intimacy
- A state of undress
- Vulnerability
- Staging potential of what's behind the curtain, in the shadows
- Long monologues
- Situational comedy
- Sight gags and physical action

Questions to Ponder/Answers to Seek:
- What staging opportunities arise from the setting—time, place, and situation?
- What are the superficial struggles that each character faces? How do these affect the internal struggles and insecurities of each character?
- How does the absurdity of the plot compliment or restrict the story?
- What elements of the play pose the most challenges for the actor(s) versus those which pose the most challenges to the director(s)?
- How does vulnerability play a role in this story and with the characters?

Feathers
a confession

Characters:

Birdie   A young woman. Her full name is Bernadette.

Max   A young man.

Setting   A bathroom. The morning after.

> *PRODUCTION NOTE: Feel free to change the poet and actor references. Director also has permission to substitute "Chuck Norris DVD" with any gratuitous action hero junk.*

> *A large fashionable bathroom. AT RISE, we see the steamed glass door (or curtain) to a walk-in shower and the humming of a very happy young woman, BIRDIE. We can see the shadow of her as she sings and dances to her own song. After a minute or so, MAX enters in his underwear. He moves to the sink and peers into the mirror. He seems invigorated from a great night's sleep. He reaches for his toothbrush and toothpaste and turns on the water to brush his teeth. The moment he speaks, the singing and shadowy movement behind the steam stops.*

MAX: (*almost serenading her*) Good morning. (*silence*) I said goooood moorning, Beautiful.

BIRDIE: (*nervously, with a slight giggle*) Max?

MAX: Well, yes, of course. Who else would it be? Good morning, Sunshine.

BIRDIE: Oh. Good morning. My dad used to call me sunshine.

MAX: Oh. Probably not the best image to create after last night, huh? Maybe, good morning, lover. Or hot stuff. Or Bernie. Or—

BIRDIE: Birdie. It's a nickname. I know it's not really short for Bernadette. I like beautiful.

MAX: Oh, I thought the bartender called you Bernie. Sorry. OK, good morning, Beautiful.

BIRDIE: (*still from behind the steamed door, a giggle*) Good morning, Handsome.

> *MAX turns on the water and begins brushing his teeth.*

MAX: (*with a mouthful of paste and brush*) Ah hoop yoo shlooop woo?

BIRDIE: Hmm? I'm sorry. Oh, did I sleep well? I did. Very. Thank you.

> *BIRDIE turns off the water. The shower door (curtain) slides open slightly. She peeks out, looking for her towel. It's slightly out of reach. She looks over at MAX who turns and smiles sweetly to her as he continues to brush his teeth.*

BIRDIE: Are you going to be long?

MAX: (*spits*) Almost done.

> *BIRDIE slides back into the shower, closes the door (curtain). MAX finishes brushing his teeth, rinses his mouth, then moves to the shower to join her with an impish grin. BIRDIE grabs the handle of the door (curtain) to hold it in place.*

BIRDIE: What are you doing?

MAX: I was going to join you, Beautiful.

BIRDIE: No. Ummm, I'm not dressed.

MAX: (*giggling a bit*) Why, yes, I know. That's most of the reason I was going to join you.

> *He attempts to join her again. BIRDIE again prevents the door (curtain) from opening.*

BIRDIE: I would prefer you not. . . . Sweetie. Max.

MAX: (*confused*) Bernadette? Birdie? Is everything OK?

BIRDIE: (*hesitantly trying to come up with a satisfactory answer*) Yes. Everything is . . . great. Fantastic. Awesome. I had a really great time last night. You know . . . the sex and all. The sex was great. And the company. You. You were . . . well . . . great. Amazing. Great.

MAX: Oh, well . . . great. I guess. But today, this morning? Not so great?

BIRDIE: No, you're still . . . well, I woke up this morning and you were lying there so peacefully. Just looking like a perfect man. So handsome. So warm. So damned gorgeous I wanted to take a bite out of you. But I thought after last night, I . . . well, after what we did . . . and did . . . and well, you know, the sex. The great sex. It was mind-blowing actually. I thought I would probably clean up, take a quick shower while you slept.

MAX smiles, incredibly flattered, even impressed with himself.

MAX: Oh, of course. Of course. Take a shower. My house is your house. What's mine is yours. Make yourself at home. You were amazing as well. I mean, you still are. That's why I don't want you to go. That's why I wanted to join you. I thought I would, you know, continue what we started last night. I always dreamed of this. Waking up, showering together. Never done that before. Thought this might be a nice first.

BIRDIE: A nice first? Maybe. Maybe not. I'm . . . hesitant. I'm not sure you're ready or I'm ready.

MAX: Hesitant? Ready? For what? I'm ready for anything, Bernadette. I thought last night was one of those rarities. I don't really bring women back to my apartment.

BIRDIE: (*she peeks out again*)   Oh, of course not. I wasn't saying, implying that. I'm not sure I'm ready. I really had a great time last night and I don't want you to get the wrong impression. I really, REALLY enjoyed myself. It was magical.

MAX: Magical. I'll take magical, but it doesn't have to end. Let's keep it going.

MAX starts for the shower once more.

BIRDIE: (*stopping him again*)   What are you doing?

MAX: Joining you.

BIRDIE: Wait! Wait. Wait.

MAX: You don't want to?

BIRDIE: No, that's not it. That's really not it at all. I REALLY want to . . . but . . .

MAX: Come on, Bernadette. Beautiful. Brace yourself. I'm coming in.

> BIRDIE *nervously moves back into the shower. We see her shadow move to the back as MAX steps in. We see his underwear come off as he tosses them over the door (curtain) and turns to her. We now see their silhouettes.*

MAX: Bernadette, I—

BIRDIE: Yes?

MAX: Wh . . . wh . . .

> *MAX screams.*

MAX: What? What is that? What are those?!

BIRDIE: Feathers.

MAX: Feathers?!

BIRDIE: I can explain. Wait. Before you freak out.

MAX: Feathers?! Feathers? What? Feathers?! You have feathers? Down there?

> *The door (curtain)   opens. MAX reaches out for the towel hanging outside the door, wraps himself in it, and jumps out of the shower.*

MAX: Oh my God. Oh my God. Oh my God.

BIRDIE: (*peeking out of the door, searching*)   Could you hand me a towel please? I'd like to talk about this before you run out of the room screaming.

MAX: (*not very convincingly*)   Run out of the room? Who's running? I'm fine. I'm great. The woman I just spent the best night of my life with, the woman who I had dreams of having the greatest sex of my life with after a night of having the greatest sex of my life, turns out to be half . . .

MAX hands her a towel from another rack. BIRDIE wraps herself in one and steps out of the shower.

BIRDIE: Swan.

MAX: Half-swan? You're half-swan. I had a one-night stand with a swan.

BIRDIE: Half-swan. "I had the greatest night of my life with a half-swan" would be more accurate. And I did too. It was just amazing, Max. Everything. The talks, the dinner, the dancing, the sex, just the connection we made.

MAX: No, yeah, it was nice. I guess.

BIRDIE: "I guess?" Now that you know this, it's "nice"? But before it was "the greatest"—

MAX: Well, look, it just took me by surprise that's all. I mean, I don't remember seeing . . . feeling feathers down there.

BIRDIE: They were there. I just thought you knew and you didn't care. Like you didn't mind that I was different. That what we had was more than that.

MAX: It was. It is. I mean, before . . . I thought you were like me. But not like me. Better than what I deserved even. I just . . . This is a lot to take in. You have to agree. I never expected feathers. I think maybe I thought you were different and things were going so well that I feared . . . I mean, my track record hasn't been that great with women and I tend to be a bit pessimistic. I thought, "You're going to blow this, Max. Look at this great, attractive, intelligent, funny woman. You two are hitting it off. Things are going so well. She said yes to coming back to my apartment. That means she may be into me. I have a shot here, at something. At some meaningless sex or a second date even better. Or something that I may be longing for, someone I could spend time with, cook breakfast for, shower with even. But you're going to say something wrong, Max. Or maybe she isn't a she. What if she's got a penis?" And at some point, we connected and I didn't even care anymore. I thought, "OK. If she's got a penis, I'll deal with that. I can adjust even. Maybe.

Maybe this connection is real. Maybe I'm gay. Maybe I'm something else entirely! Maybe all of this confusion and fear of being alone or isolated is because I put up walls and restrictions. Maybe that's it. Maybe I should just go with it, you know. Maybe the hell with overthinking and analyzing. Just be you, Max. Just try and connect with her. Have fun. Who cares? This person in front of me. We're starting a journey. And this connection doesn't happen to everyone. But it's happening now. I don't care if Bernadette has a penis. Or a vagina. Or both. I don't care." But feathers. I never expected feathers. I expected human. Not swan. Not feathers.

BIRDIE: Half-swan. I'm half-human too. And it was the same for me. I felt that too. I didn't care if you were all human. I didn't care.

MAX: Is there some sort of stigma to being all human?!

BIRDIE: That's not what I meant. You didn't notice anything last night? Didn't feel anything?

MAX: No! I didn't, believe me.

BIRDIE: Maybe you did and it didn't matter?

MAX: I think I would have known if I had felt feathers.

BIRDIE: Are you sure? They are very soft.

MAX: I would know.

BIRDIE: You want me to go. I'll go. I understand. The feathers are a bit shocking.

MAX: Well, yes. Of course they are. Wouldn't they be?

BIRDIE: I wouldn't know, Max. I've never shown them to anyone before!

MAX: You wouldn't know? Oh. But you were so good. We did all sort of things. Really amazing things. How did you know what to do if . . .

BIRDIE: Because I knew being like this was probably going to be a big obstacle to having sex. I thought I should research things. I read books, magazines. I've seen movies. (*embarrassed*)   I may have watched a porn or two. I wanted to be good at it. You know, just in case.

MAX: Well, you were. The sex was . . .

BIRDIE: Mind-blowing? (*taking his silence for a "yes"*) Oh good. I did it right. Phew. Because you were . . . well, you were "grrr" and "come here" and "take this!" and loving, sweet then rough and scary . . . and . . . phew. I mean PHEW! Let's just say you blew my feathers off. I had to take that shower. And cool off.

MAX: Thank you.

BIRDIE: So you want me to go?

MAX: I don't know. I have questions.

BIRDIE: OK, ask.

MAX: I mean I don't want to offend you. I just don't know how to frame it, how to ask.

BIRDIE: Just say it. Ask me anything. I'll tell you the truth.

MAX: Feathers . . . anywhere else?

BIRDIE: Nope. Just there. Everything else as far as I know is just like every other woman. Perfectly normal. Other women lay eggs, right?

MAX: What?

BIRDIE: I'm kidding, Max. No, I promise. No more surprises. None. I have feathers down there. But I fell for a guy last night and so I did it. It. I did it, feathers and all, and I held nothing back. I just wanted to be with him. I knew there would be that time, that moment when someone would know. I would have to choose to show my secret. And unfortunately, it would be at that most intimate of times. The deed. The joining. The dirty dance.

MAX: What about checkups? Going to a doctor? Or gym class?

BIRDIE: Mom's a doctor. Doctor's notes.

MAX: Oh, well, if you're going to have feathers, that's convenient. And you were born that way? It's not contagious?

BIRDIE: Would that matter?

MAX: (*after a moment*)   No, not really. I guess not. Right at this moment I wish I had feathers.

BIRDIE: Aww, that is so sweet, Max.

> *She starts to move to him. MAX takes a breath and may even step back slightly.*

MAX: Just a sec. Give me a minute.

BIRDIE: Max, I'm here. I have feathers. And you need to decide whether that's OK for you. Does that matter to you? I had feathers last night when you bought me that drink, when we talked about Hitchcock movies and how we both hate Casablanca, and I had feathers when we had sex last night on the kitchen table, in the living room, and in the closet and even in your bed. I have feathers. But I don't care that you don't have feathers. That you're not covered in them. When I was a kid, I actually thought that was going to be my Prince Charming. A giant swan with man legs, covered in feathers, wearing a crown, riding his white horse. That feathered Prince would be the one who liked my feathers. He would say, "You're like nothing I've ever seen and that is why I love you." You don't have to be that prince, Max. I just wanted a nice date and maybe a satisfying night of sex. If there's more, then get in this shower with me. Feathers and all. Do you still hate Casablanca?

MAX: Yes.

BIRDIE: Do you still love Hitchcock?

MAX: Yes.

BIRDIE: Do you still want to read romance novels with me and reenact the hot scenes?

MAX: Yes, maybe. Yes.

BIRDIE: I'm going to turn on this shower, get in there, lose this towel, and finish what I was doing. You are welcome to join me. Do you still think the poetry of Maya Angelou is indulgent bilge and that Bruce Willis may be the most underrated actor of our age?

MAX: Yes.

BIRDIE eases into the shower and turns it on. After a moment, MAX steps in as well. Both towels are tossed out. We see their silhouettes slowly move toward each other.

MAX: (*continuing, trying to give her something*)   I once stole a Chuck Norris DVD* from Walmart because I just had to have it but was ashamed to pay five dollars for it.

BLACKOUT. END OF PLAY.

❧ Masterpiece ❧

Two people: one male, one female or a couple; a simple set: a stool and an easel.

Anton has taken up painting, and with the light fading and a deadline looming, he asks his wife to model for him. She has other ideas.

Page-to-Stage Challenges:

- Physical intimacy and vulnerability
- A state of undress
- Adult subject matter or themes
- Comic visual contrasts
- Very static staging that must be addressed
- Creative solutions for the "nudity"
- An exploration of what isn't said

Questions to Ponder/Answers to Seek:

- How do the goals of each character compliment or resist the other?
- What obstacles pose the greatest threat to each character's main objective?
- How does vulnerability manifest itself with each character and how does each character deal with it or overcome it?
- How does each character deal with the familiar versus the unfamiliar in the play?

Masterpiece

a project

Characters:

Anton   The husband who's recently taken up painting.

Molly   The wife, his reluctant subject.

Setting   Anton's studio.

PRODUCTION NOTES: The "nudity" should be the least important thing about the play. Feel free to suggest instead of show. Creative costumes and/or lighting might work best. Atmosphere is more important than getting an accurate set. A simple easel, stool, and a pool of light would work. Also, background music underscoring the pretentiousness of Anton's workspace may play such as Billy Joel's "Waltz No. 1 (Nunley's Carousel)" and "Invention in C Minor."

> *AT RISE, ANTON sits behind an easel, brush and paint in hand, classical music playing softly. Opposite him, we see MOLLY in a robe standing next to a tall stool in a beam of light from a large window on the other side of the room. ANTON studies her and occasionally puts brush to canvas. MOLLY seems uneasy in the robe.*

ANTON: OK, hold still. Just a bit more.

MOLLY: (*sighing*)   How much longer?

ANTON: Honey, you have to stand perfectly still. I need to get the shading correct and if you move, it screws up the entire perspective.

MOLLY: Sorry.

ANTON: Just hold still a moment more.

MOLLY: Am I going to get to see it soon?

ANTON: Just a minute longer. No, the hands aren't right. Forget the hands. I just won't do hands.

MOLLY: I'm not going to have any hands?

> *ANTON glares at her briefly to hold still. MOLLY stands as still as her patience will allow. She tries to subtly blow a piece of hair out of her eyes. She fails and blows again.*

ANTON: Molly!

MOLLY: I'm sorry. When I agreed to do this, I thought this was going to be more . . . sexy. More fun.

ANTON: It will be. Just one more second.

MOLLY: One more second. One more minute. Jesus. Anton, this is not what I had in mind.

ANTON: OK, got it. Now. Lose the robe.

MOLLY: Lose the robe? Just like that?

ANTON: Just like that.

MOLLY: *(playfully)* No foreplay?

ANTON: Honey.

MOLLY: OK. OK. God, this is nothing like I thought it would be. What are you painting anyway? First with clothes then without? I agreed to do this because I wanted to be supportive.

ANTON: You are. You are being incredibly supportive. Now lose the robe.

MOLLY: Seriously, Anton. So like are you going to hang this in our bedroom or is it part of an exhibit? Can I see it?

ANTON: You are never going to see it and it's an assignment. An experimental piece. The whole thing sort of evolves. One pose morphing into another. I want it to reflect all of you. I had to capture the face first. The eyes. Now I move onto the body. So if you would please . . .

MOLLY: OK. OK.

> *MOLLY drops her robe to reveal that she is wearing a negligee and lacy panties.*

ANTON: Molly. Really? This is a nude portrait. You said you were comfortable with that.

MOLLY: Yes, I was. I am. But I thought that was just an excuse to get me naked so we could . . . you know. Have fun. (*pause*)   What do you mean I'm never going to see it?

ANTON: I just can't, Molly. It's not finished. And even then—Look, I need you to be completely nude for this painting to work so if you're not comfortable, I can get another model.

MOLLY: What?! No. I'll do it. I don't want you to replace me with anyone else. I'll do it.

ANTON: (*indicating her lacy underwear*)   So. Lose the . . .

MOLLY: It's a negligee, Anton. And it's new.

ANTON: Well, it's beautiful. Now, I have a lot of work to do here.

MOLLY: Can't you even ask me in a nicer way? Make it sexy or something?

ANTON: Honey, this painting is not sexy. It's a portrait of something primal. A raw emotion. Exposed. Possibly shocking.

MOLLY: That doesn't sound sexy.

ANTON: No, well, it's not supposed to.

MOLLY: I want to look sexy. I want others to look at it and covet your wife.

ANTON: That's not what this is about. Honey, we're losing the natural light from the window. Are you in or out?

MOLLY: I'm in. OK. Jesus. Do you treat all of your models this way?

ANTON: That's not fair. You know that's not fair. This is my first attempt at something human. I chose you because, well, my teacher said I couldn't paint any more fruit and no landscapes. He definitely made that clear. That's another class.

MOLLY: You're going to show this to your teacher? That's weird and a little creepy.

ANTON:	He's a professional artist, Molly. He's very accustomed to the naked body. Now, please, Honey, lose the underwear.
MOLLY:	All of this talking has really killed the mood for me.
ANTON:	Good. Now get naked.
MOLLY:	Good?
ANTON:	Yeah. Don't think of this as sexy time or fun time. This is business, Molly. This is my art. I need a naked body for my art.
MOLLY:	I liked you more when you were painting fruit.

ANTON stares at MOLLY begging for a concession. After a brief silent standoff, MOLLY begins to undo her top, but she turns her back to ANTON, playfully trying to rekindle something.

ANTON:	What are you doing?
MOLLY:	Getting naked for my man. You want to see?
ANTON:	Molly, I've seen you naked before. Now, come on, before we lose the light and you're going to have to lose the bottoms too.
MOLLY:	Um, I didn't . . . um, I probably should have shaved . . . more. It's like a rain forest down there right now.
ANTON:	Honey, it doesn't matter.
MOLLY:	To you maybe. But if people are going to see me completely bare then I want to look good. If I take all of this off, will you fix some things?
ANTON:	Fix things? Fix what?
MOLLY:	You know, groom me . . . down there. Fix my imperfections on the canvas.
ANTON:	Fix your . . . what imperfections?
MOLLY:	Well, for one thing, my boobs are uneven.
ANTON:	No, they're not. They're fine.
MOLLY:	They're uneven, Anton. You've never noticed that my boobs are different sizes? One is a C and the other is almost a D.

ANTON: Honey, this is crazy. Your boobs are fine. They're like beautiful ripe clusters of grapes.

MOLLY: Grapes? What the hell kind of description is that?

ANTON: It's Song of Solomon.

MOLLY: The Bible? You have a half-naked woman here and you quote the Bible?

ANTON: I was trying to be poetic and it's the first thing that came to mind. I'm sorry. The light is fading. We're really running out of time.

MOLLY: Just promise me you will fix a few things.

ANTON: Like your uneven boobs?

MOLLY: Like my boobs. And down there. Give me a nice trim.

ANTON: If you thought this was going to be sexy time, why didn't you do something with all that . . . down there?

MOLLY: Because, Anton. I did do something with that down there . . . for you. I did enough, but if I thought this was going to be on display I would have taken a bit more care. I shaved my legs. I wore a negligee. I groomed . . . a bit. When you asked me to do this, I didn't say a word. Didn't ask for anything. I'm asking for this one thing. Fix me a little! Maybe a heart shape or something. Nothing too porno though.

ANTON: OK, OK. Whatever. I will make both of your boobs D cups and I will give you a neatly groomed lawn not too porno. Whatever that means. We good? Now, please, Honey. Please take off your clothes, turn around, and pose for me on the stool.

MOLLY: C cup. Make me a C cup. And don't get frustrated. This is important. It's important to you. It's important to me.

ANTON: Whether you're a C or D cup is not important to me, Molly. Whether you have a Mondrian-inspired pubic painting between your legs is not important to me right now. What is important is that I need a naked body in this light for my project on Monday. Why is it so important to you that I correct things? This isn't plastic surgery.

MOLLY: Who's Mondrian? And it's not correcting things. But when you think of me I want you to see a little more perfection than is there. Like if I painted you, I would do the same.

ANTON: Mondrian is that guy who painted all those shapes. We saw that exhibit last month? Wait. Like what? What would you correct?

MOLLY: Well . . . I don't know. You are a little moley on your stomach.

ANTON: What? Moley?

MOLLY: Yes. You have a lot of moles. If I were going to correct something I would get rid of a few of your moles.

ANTON: You have a problem with my moles? My mom had a tanning bed when I was growing up. OK? I liked having a little pigment in my skin. I may have overdone it a bit.

MOLLY: No need to get upset.

ANTON: Who's upset? I'm not upset. We're really confessing things now. Maybe I'll just do a little more fixing on this painting. Maybe I need to take off a few pounds from around the hips.

MOLLY: Ah! You bastard. I was not criticizing you. I was just saying I want you to see me with fewer flaws.

ANTON: What flaws? I never even saw your flaws till you brought it all up.

MOLLY: But they would have come out in your painting. When you're painting, you're studying me. Every minute detail. When you're over there behind that easel and I'm over here for hours standing naked, you really get a chance to see every detail, every little mark, that's when I stop being your wife. Then I'm just a piece of fruit or a landscape. And you get to document every inch of me. And I just stand over here like a . . . dumb peach. Or a sailboat. I want you to see what you think I am not what you see I am!

ANTON: You know what? I'm not going to "fix" anything. In fact, I'm starting over.

ANTON tosses the canvas across the room then replaces it with a fresh blank canvas.

MOLLY: No, I want to see what you had there.

ANTON: No, you don't. It's terrible. Because of me. I don't have the ability to put you down on this canvas the way I see you . . . or the way you want me to see you . . . or the way you want me to think I see you. A simple stupid human hand. I CAN'T EVEN DRAW A HAND!

MOLLY: I CAN'T EVEN GET MY HUSBAND TO HAVE SEX WITH ME!

ANTON: I don't know how to paint anything else. All I've painted before this was a bowl of apples, two bananas on a paper plate, and a solitary pineapple on the dining room table.

MOLLY: On a scale of dining room pineapple to bowl of apples, how was this one coming along?

ANTON" It wasn't quite a pineapple yet, but I think it was close. I was only looking at the face before. Maybe the hands. I don't do hands well.

MOLLY forgets she's been covering her upper body with her hands and walks over to the first canvas. She picks it up and looks at the painting.

MOLLY: (*trying to comprehend what she sees but definitely not liking it*) What?— But that?—Is that my nose? Are those ears?

ANTON: Hands. They're supposed to be hands. I'm not done.

MOLLY takes the painting to ANTON's easel and replaces the blank one.

MOLLY: (*a gesture of support*) Don't start over. Just . . . you never noticed how lopsided they are? Look. Uneven. This one is much larger than this one.

ANTON: (*staring hard as if studying through a microscope*) I don't see it. (*lifting up his shirt*) I really have a lot of moles?

MOLLY: I've always thought they were cute. When you're asleep, I try to connect the dots and make pictures with them. These here form a little dog I call Reginald. (*an attempt at inspiration as she crosses downstage with the stool*)   Paint what you see. (*beat*)   Do you get grades in this class you're taking?

ANTON: Kinda. Not letter grades but he does give feedback.

MOLLY: What does he think about your fruit?

ANTON: He said Thomas Kinkade would be proud.

MOLLY: That's not a compliment, is it?

ANTON: "Uninspired and pedestrian."

MOLLY: Really? That prick. Well then, let's really shock the hell out of him.

> *She removes her underwear and sits with her back to us, putting her feet up and spreading her legs wide open to ANTON. ANTON starts to work.*

MOLLY: Once you're done, we're totally having sex.

ANTON: (*deeply concentrating on his next paint stroke*)   Mm-hmm.

> *BLACKOUT. END OF PLAY.*

⋙ Finally the Day Came
When We Had So Little to Say ⋘

Two roles: one male, one female; a single set: suggestions of a bedroom with bed, mirror, doors, etc.

Two "Greek statutes" prepare for a night out surrounded by paparazzi and adoring fans, but something sinister may be afoot as they dance around the surprises they have in store for each other at the end of the evening's festivities.

Page-to-Stage Challenges:
- Very obscure lines at times, single words, random, etc.
- Elevated language
- Long monologues
- Adult themes and language
- Vague cause-and-effect
- Lots of staging variables and prop use

Questions to Ponder/Answer to Seek:
- What is really going on between the lines?
- How does the limited dialogue open up or limit the physical choices of each character?
- What visual elements—costume, property, set, etc.—are actually needed in order to tell this story effectively?
- How does the power shift throughout the play? What choices do the characters make and how do they interact or not interact in order to maintain or take power?

Finally the Day Came
When We Had So Little to Say
a farewell

Characters:

She   A Greek statue of a woman.

He   A Greek statue of a man.

Setting   Evening. An elegant bedroom.

> *An elegant bedroom. A woman (SHE) sits at a delicate table, touching up her makeup, staring into a compact. She is dressed elegantly in a cocktail dress. Her hair is up for a formal dinner or evening soiree. A man enters (HE) also dressed formally, beautifully. They both are like sculptures, every detail finely crafted.*

SHE: Ready?

HE: Cuff links?

SHE: (*pointing to a bureau*)   Drawer.

HE: Watch.

SHE: Same.

> *HE moves to the drawer and removes the watch and cufflinks.*

HE: Ready?

SHE: Almost.

> *She moves with precision, graceful, no rush. HE is looking for something.*

HE: I—

SHE: Closet.

HE: Nothing.

SHE: Bathroom.

HE: Immaculate.

SHE: Bed.

> *He stares at her.*

SHE: (*she points to the bed*)   Under.

HE: No—

SHE: Look.

> *He looks under the bed. He retrieves a small briefcase and holds it up to show her.*

HE: No.

SHE: Oh.

> *SHE points toward another part of the house. HE exits in that direction. SHE continues to touch up her makeup quietly. Her moves are precise and delicate. After a moment, HE returns with a different briefcase. His search is over.*

HE: Dinner?

SHE: Briefly.

HE: After.

SHE: Here.

> *HE stares off for a moment.*

SHE: Chicken.

> *HE turns and smirks at her. Then he glides toward her, moves in behind her and kisses her neck gently.*

HE: Nope.

SHE: Cad.

HE: Cad?

> *She glares at him. A flirt or a threat?*

HE: I surrender.

SHE: (*laughing incredulously*)   My soulmate. My—

HE: Unrelenting love.

SHE: (*a brutal laughter*)   Don't make me—

HE: Our lives are—

SHE: (*correcting him*)   Have become.

HE: A maze, a puzzle . . .

SHE: Asbestos and ash.

HE: The theatre misses you.

SHE: As the gutter, you.

A pause. HE reflects.

HE: So it's clear. After dinner.

SHE: Back here. You will undress me.

HE: And you me. Slowly. Painlessly.

SHE: Leave the briefcase outside.

HE: Take your garters off before.

They share a look.

SHE: I'm going to end this.

HE: Not before I do. Finally.

SHE: Dinner should be without a fracture. Without suspicion.

HE: When have I ever disappointed or failed in my role?

SHE: I lose count when I'm bored or being fucked.

A beat.

HE   The claws are out early. It's as if you suffer preshow jitters, like an amateur. Shall we wait?

SHE: Your reticence reminds me of an eighteen-year-old French boy fumbling his zipper in one hand and my bra clasp in the other.

HE: What ever happened to 'enri? The last I remember he went missing in the winter after a rather large helping of bouillabaisse. Such a cliché really. A dime store novella if I ever heard one.

SHE: Must I remind you who wrote it? And it was spring. Old age too much for you?

HE: You have managed. That dress hides the flaws beautifully. Like a checkered tablecloth on a folding card table.

SHE: (*laughs*)   And you see, this. This is why we make such a great couple. Like oil and water. Fire and Ice.

HE: Arsenic and old lace. (*beat.*)   It's funny, isn't it? How the games we play always end up going there. Toward the darkness. I don't recall the moment it changed. Was it a moment in time? A season? Where one suddenly looks around and the leaves have changed and you don't recognize the world anymore? You don't recognize yourself. You barely recognize that you're awake. And you know what? (*a change comes over him, the sculpture cracks*)   It really pisses me off. How was I, how were we supposed to see this? Did you dream of this? In the deepest recess of your brain does this thought reside somewhere? Incessancy? Inevitability! I scream for you. I pine for you. You weep for me. You never EVER undress me with your eyes. I get to touch you. I GET to touch you. Like an allowance. And I'm just as guilty for the assumption that you want the same things. That we're in the same boat. But . . . I don't know now.

> SHE *walks over to him and presents the back of her dress, asking for a hand with the zipper. HE assists, kisses her neck almost like a ritual, and then continues his rant.*

HE: (*continued*)   Maybe I did once, but I don't know now. I CAN'T READ YOUR MIND! And this is the moment where I'm supposed to say I HATE YOU! I HATE YOU! But I don't say this. The thought has never crossed my mind. I want hate to fuel all of this. A hydroelectric power plant of hate. But no. I HATE ME. At least I think I hate me. As much as Narcissus hates a reflecting pool. I hate that I said that. Damn it.

> HE *crosses hard toward the bathroom door, so quickly that his shoe comes off. SHE sighs. HE retrieves his shoe.*

SHE: Your shoe.

HE: I know. My shoe.

SHE: (*singsong*) Tawdry, tawdry, never got his way. Sins and secrets did him in that day.

HE: Is that supposed to be funny? Or insightful?

SHE: I'll let you decide. You poor, poor man. About an hour ago I took a pill. A pretty little yellow pill. An hour before that I took a blue pill. And then an hour before that a pill of deep red. My own little rainbow. I am always amazed at how high I can get and still function normally. The red allows me to dive into my lingerie bureau. The blue allows me to shower and dress afterward. The yellow one keeps me from committing a crime. About this time of day, when I've completely disregarded the warning labels on the little bottles, I feel so powerful. I feel so capable. The instinct is not survival but of responsibility to the whole. My existence has purpose. Our presence, when we step out of this room, when people see us, they feel fed yet vanquished. Like a religious ecstasy. The flashes of cameras, the microphones, the red carpets, the POP! . . . arazzi. Like we're the only thing in their lives that has meaning. We have a duty to give them what they really want. Not what they think they want or tell people they want. What they are so ashamed to admit. Give them false aspirations. Wink at someone in the crowd. Let your fingers just brush the adoring outstretched fingers. That is importance. That is calling. We are shaping minds. We give meaning to an angry, hopeless, confused mass who only want to know one thing: am I like you? Is there any greater goal? We are Jesus for the believers and Beyonce for everyone else. And to think you want to waste one sparked neuron of thought on what my feelings are about you or us or hate or love? Get it together, man.

HE: Maybe ending this pony show is the right move. There will be headlines. So many photographs and interviews to pull quotes. Their imaginations will run wild.

SHE: You're thinking so small. This will break them. Social media? The news? This will determine the future. Headlines? We write cultural scripture. You're thinking small. And that isn't worthy of this room, these clothes. You aren't worthy of my flesh. Flaccid. If you want this body, you have to break something.

HE: What about the children? Audrey and Supreme? How will they look at the world? Will they find a course?

SHE: (*laughing again*)   They will set the course. Supreme will write songs. Audrey will run for President. The melodies will pine for us to return. The speeches will hail us as innovators. We are the God's breath that people crave.

HE: Of course you're right. As I walk out this door, I should like to take a knife and plunge it into the first person I see.

SHE: I wouldn't blame you a bit. You'd never see a jail cell. It's wrong of course. At least ten people not including Audrey would rise in your defense.

HE: I shouldn't burden them with that. They have enough going on. The reactions we got when we entertained adopting that immigrant child.

SHE: Enough talk. Time for action.

HE: To moustache or not to moustache?

> HE has pulled out a small case that he opens and we see a wide variety of moustaches laid out like a jewelry collection.

SHE: To.

HE: And you're going with those eyes?

SHE: You don't like the brown?

HE: I think it's a big mistake not going with the green.

SHE: (*standing her ground*)   I think brown.

HE: (*defiantly*)   Then no moustache.

SHE: After dinner then?

HE: Straight back here.

SHE: And then a Picasso!

HE: He should be so lucky.

SHE: You've returned to me.

HE: Never left. Detoured.

SHE: I envy them.

HE: I as well.

SHE: I'll leave first.

HE: (*indicating himself*)   Five minutes later.

SHE: Ta-ta.

> *SHE begins to exit.*

HE: A moment!

> *HE moves to her and dabs her skin at the temple as if repairing it.*

SHE: You're welcome.

> *A beat. A decision. SHE goes to her nightstand and retrieves something forgotten. Turning away from us, she raises her skirt and hides something in a garter or somewhere else.*

SHE: (*finishing her routine*)   Well, all—

HE: Set? Yes.

SHE: That is . . .

HE: That. Yes.

SHE: Gloves.

HE: (*handing gloves to her*)   Gloves.

SHE: Gloves?

HE: (*indicating his*)   Gloves.

SHE: Goodbye.

> *SHE exits. HE moves to drawer and removes something exceptionally violent looking. A weapon? A mask? A scandal?*

HE: If . . .

> *HE exits. BLACKOUT. END OF PLAY.*

✒ Lyla Builds a Spaceship ✒

Two people: one male, one female; a simple set: two sitting positions.

Seeking absolution for years of womanizing and reckless behavior, Hal seeks out the sister of a girl from his past only to be engaged in the oddest of construction projects.

Page-to-Stage Challenges:

- A kissing scene
- Odd noncasual dialogue and interruptions
- Lots of backstory revealed
- Lots of staging opportunities—very flexible
- Playing with property

Questions to Ponder/Answers to Seek:

- How do the contrasts in each character's ultimate goal affect the relationship and story progression?
- How do the power dynamics shift throughout the play?
- What visual elements are necessary for the story to be told effectively?
- What common goals do the characters share?
- What role does the spaceship play for each character?

Lyla Builds a Spaceship
a deconstruction

Characters:

Lyla   Mid-twenties, detached from the world either by choice or circumstance. She speaks playfully, but with pointed accuracy, living with one foot in this world and one foot in a far-off place.

Hal   Mid-twenties to early thirties, well dressed, a product of good breeding now seeking something he touched years ago. Too serious for his age.

Setting   A courtyard of a rest home or facility.

> *LYLA, in a brightly colored spring dress, sits on a blanket amid random scraps of cardboard and metal, an assortment of things she has collected. She works on something large which resembles little more than cardboard, metal, and silver tape. She is a focused engineer surrounded by grass, a bush or two, maybe a bench, moving purposefully, only occasionally pausing to survey her work. HAL enters.*

HAL: Excuse me. Lyla?

> *LYLA gives him a short glance then turns back to her work.*

HAL: I'm looking for Lyla. The man at the desk said I'd find her out here. The nurse over there pointed me to you. She said the one you're looking for is that girl tinkering away. Your project?

> *HAL thinks he's made a mistake. Then she stops but doesn't look his way.*

LYLA: Interruptions. (*referring to her work*) I've got to get that smoother or . . .

HAL: Oh. I'll help?

LYLA: Duct tape.

HAL: Excuse me?

LYLA: Duct tape.

HAL: Oh. Yes. I'm sure it's around here somewhere.

> *HAL searches superficially, not sure he should disturb the piled madness before him. After a moment or two, LYLA reaches over and plucks it up as if she knew where it was all along, rips off several strips and begins patching random areas and fastening things to her cardboard project.*

HAL: Ah, there it is. Right in front of my nose.

> *He laughs hoping this may start to engage her. It does not.*

LYLA: (*not stopping her project*)   Your name's Hal. Ten years ago, you had a fling with my sister, Amanda. Ten days of nice conversations, flirtations, and companionship. She fell for you. You never returned her call after that last night. That one night. I believe intercourse was involved. Her first orgasm, as I recall. Not your first.

> *LYLA continues her work, seemingly unaffected. After recovering from the blunt assessment, he continues.*

HAL: Oh. Wow. She told you all that?

LYLA: She tells me everything. Even your description down to your dimpled cheek and the size of your penis. Which leans to the left I believe. Every Wednesday evening and other Saturday. She brings '80s music and Star Trek films. Last week she brought the films of John Hughes for a change. Interesting but juvenile and predictable. Shortsighted. I prefer Star Trek. The original film, director's cut. The latest one is quite good. Inventive, and—

HAL: Yes, it is, I guess. I'm sorry to interrupt, but I was wondering, well . . . I just wanted to know if you'd . . . if you'd heard . . . from Mandy, your sister?

> *LYLA stands, surveying her progress. She plucks a leaf from a nearby bush then eats it like she's eating from a bowl of popcorn.*

HAL: That's probably not good for you.

LYLA: Mentha piperita.

HAL: Uhhh—

LYLA: Chocolate mint.

HAL: (*laughing*)   It is? Like ice cream? The bush? Sure.

LYLA: (*regarding her project*) Something's missing. How to overcome the atmospheric friction. . . . Think, Lyla.

> *LYLA grabs another leaf, eats it. She gets an idea and goes back to work.*

HAL: It took some time to track you down. I've been looking for your sister for some time, phone books, online, but it's been so long. I figured she'd moved but I remember her saying she had a sister, Lyla. I remembered your name. Lyla. And that Mandy said she lived here. At this place. Not at home. Mandy never said why. Could you stop that for a minute?

LYLA: You seek Amanda. She's not here. I haven't seen her at all this week. Absent on Wednesday and a no-show yesterday as well. Gave me time to work. I enjoy our visits but I find that they do take time away from research.

HAL: Your research? A cardboard box? Or a cardboard something. What is that?

> *LYLA turns to him as if to reveal it then changes her mind, grabs another leaf, eats it then continues working.*

LYLA: Amanda is not here. If you seek an orgasm, you won't find it here. I am involved in something at the moment.

HAL: No, that's not what I seek. (*sighs*)   This is a bad idea. I just thought . . . Could I leave a note? Maybe she'll show up. You could give it to her.

LYLA: If I'm here, I could. Though I don't think she will want your note.

HAL: You're probably right. If she told you that, she probably told you a lot worse. Colored me very appropriately. I'm not going to make excuses for the past. I was an ass. Played around a lot. A lot of women. Parties. Fun stuff, I guess. Well, it's not important. I just wanted to say I'm sorry to her. For some of the things I did. Sort of a thing I'm doing, a sort of self-imposed walk. I promised myself I'd try to fix some things.

LYLA: Mandy is not here. She wasn't here on Wednesday and she wasn't here yesterday.

HAL: Yeah, I gotcha. I'm sorry to interrupt. I just didn't know who to talk to. Your mother, maybe? I could find her.

LYLA: Good luck. That's going to be an expensive phone call.

HAL: She live abroad? Doesn't matter. I'd really like to find Mandy. Talk to her. Money's no expense really.

LYLA: My mother left five years ago.

> LYLA peers into the sky briefly.

HAL: Oh. I'm sorry. I didn't know.

LYLA: (*as if confused by his apology*)   It wasn't your idea. Sometimes our minds are strong but our bodies are weak. Sometimes it's the other way around. My mother was the other way around. She left her body intact though. More duct tape.

HAL: Duct tape? Ah, I got this.

> HAL goes for the duct tape and then starts to notice all the bits of metal and random wires and utensils.

LYLA: (*referring to a piece of metal that looks a lot like a mixer blade*)   Please be careful with those components. That particular piece you're about to stand on is very difficult to find. It may hold the key to this entire project's success.

HAL: Duct tape. A miracle invention, isn't it?

LYLA: Correct. Few people understand its potential usages.

HAL: I know people who make wallets out of it, clothes even. In college, there's no telling what all I used it for.

LYLA: No, you didn't.

HAL: Pardon?

LYLA: You knew Mandy. Mandy made wallets and clothes out of duct tape. Mandy knew people who made wallets and clothes out of duct tape. Your hands are soft, manicured. You spent approximately $1,200 on your ensemble. I believe that watch is Tag Heuer, retail approximately $3,300. $150 on the haircut and styling gel, vanilla and palm scented. You have no friends who use duct tape. The attempt to continue the conversation is thoughtful, but unnecessary. If you wish to remain here and observe, you can. You may even help. Just make sure you are clear at takeoff and tell them you had no idea what I was doing. Say you were coerced.

HAL: (*laughing politely*)   Takeoff? You building a rocket?

LYLA: Actually, no. The rocket was the first step. After the initial tests were successful, I decided the natural next step was an orbital objective. Then who knows.

HAL: So that's why you're here.

LYLA: That's why I'm here. It's a place where I can think and work in peace.

HAL: Ah. Not because you build rockets and spaceships out of cardboard and you think that it's somehow going to propel you into space? Doesn't that sound a bit . . . (*not wanting to say "crazy"*)   far-fetched?

LYLA: It is far-fetched. Crazy even.

>   *She plucks another leaf and eats it. She offers one to HAL who politely declines.*

LYLA: (*continued*)   But given time, all good ideas seemingly crazy at first often become springboards for great things, life-changing, culture changing events. Magellan, Columbus, explorers all thought to be far-fetched in their pie-in-the-sky goals. Then came Armstrong and Aldrin. Kirk and Picard.

HAL: I don't think those last two are real.

LYLA: (*pausing briefly, then dismissing him*)   Who knew duct tape would save an Apollo crew? That an industrial glue would become Post-It Notes?

HAL: Wasn't the Post-It Note a failed experiment? He didn't mean to make it or something?

LYLA: (*impressed with his point*)   Very good. But even mistakes have proven important. Silly Putty, cheese, chocolate chip cookies. All mistakes.

HAL: But those don't kill you. If you don't make cheese, you don't burn up in the atmosphere or plummet to your death.

LYLA: That is very true.

> *LYLA continues to work. HAL decides to help.*

HAL: I shouldn't have lied. Frankly, I don't know why I did.

LYLA: You're trying to find a reason to stay, to keep talking. You don't need one. Just don't get in the way.

HAL: I won't.

> *As a gesture, he walks over and plucks a leaf. After sniffing it, he sticks it in his mouth then hesitantly chews.*

HAL: Hey, it does taste a bit like mint. Weird.

LYLA: Of course. I'm not crazy. Who would just reach out and start gnawing on some random tree? Mentha piperita. Citrata, to be specific. Technically. Chocolate mint. (*conceding*)   Or orange mint. There is a lot of disagreement on that one. Some people make tea out of it. I'm sure the people here don't know what they've got. Probably planted it by accident. There isn't another one around. Happy accidents. A mistake. See?

HAL: (*relaxing a bit*)   To be honest, I don't know where I'd go.

LYLA: I find that hard to believe. You are attractive, probably rich, a sense of style. Intercourse should be easy for you.

HAL: (*not happy about the admission*)   You'd think. Yeah, I guess it is. It's always been easy.

LYLA: Do you find me attractive?

HAL: I'm not sure we should be talking about this. Here. I came to find Mandy. Your sister.

LYLA: When you first entered, I felt your eyes on me. Approximately seven seconds surveying my body before you spoke. I assume you were looking at certain areas, my legs, my breasts. Three seconds on the legs, four or five on the breasts. They are accentuated by this dress. Maybe that's why Mandy gave it to me.

HAL: I was not . . . I may have been. I'm sorry. I wasn't expecting you to look the way you do. A lot like her. From behind. When I came out here and first saw you. For a moment I hoped it was her.

LYLA: I'm sorry to disappoint you. But I appreciate the honesty and the seven seconds.

HAL: (*confused*)   OK. You too. I don't get this brutal honesty. It's a little refreshing.

LYLA: There was an accident. Amanda was in an accident.

HAL: Wait. What?

LYLA: That's why she didn't come this week.

HAL: Oh, my gosh. Uh, was she hurt? Is she in the hospital?

LYLA peers into the sky once more.

LYLA: No. I think I'm going to need more weight. The oddity of flight is that you need a critical weight for control. Too little weight and you are at the mercy of wind currents and propulsion needs a little something to push.

HAL: Is that why you're building this ship? To get up there? Near her?

LYLA: Why are you trying to find Amanda?

HAL: I told you. I didn't like myself back then. I don't like myself much now. I'm trying to come to terms with some things. It's a long story. Call it a bucket list of sorts. Wishful thinking maybe.

LYLA: Well, the ship only carries one person. It's a prototype.

HAL: The ship? This thing? This mass of cardboard and duct tape and kitchen utensils?! That's not a real rocket ship. You're not an astronaut or whatever. You're in the courtyard of a— (*stopping himself*)

LYLA: Is this how you hurt women? Congratulations, Hal. You're batting the proverbial thousand.

HAL: No. Look, I'm sorry. But you have got to see this isn't going to work.

> *Without any indication, LYLA leaps at HAL and kisses him. HAL is taken off guard and pushes her off of him.*

HAL: What the hell are you doing?

LYLA: Still breaking hearts, aren't you, Hal?

HAL: I, uh, I don't know what you think you're doing but I just came hoping to find Mandy. Or someone who knows Mandy. Or something.

LYLA: (*smiling*)   I wanted to reward you for trying to save me. It was adorable. Arousing. This is very dangerous work but rest assured I've taken all the necessary precautions. There is no reward without great risk.

HAL: I wasn't trying to . . . I mean I'm just saying that you know that thing will never . . .

> *Before he can finish his thought, LYLA leaps for him again, kissing him harder this time, grabbing his hands and placing them on her body, trying to put them in the most inappropriate of places, finishing with a hard clutch of his rear with both hands.*

HAL: (*muffled from Lyla's attack*)   What are . . . this . . . please stop.

> *HAL finally manages to pull her off of him. LYLA giggles. HAL looks around for help.*

LYLA: No one is coming. They don't really pay attention to me. "Harmless." I'm sure they mentioned that. Do you think I could get away with a rocket test flight and the construction of this module if they were always watching me?

HAL: Why did you do that?

LYLA: (*giggling again*)   I'm an explorer. I need to discover things. Call it a test flight. And I found it arousing that you would try to save me. And now that I think about it, what if I succeed in breaking the earth's bonds? I will need someone to help me populate some far-off place, a young planet, a distant moon. I will need another's DNA. Yours would suffice.

HAL: Save you? I'm not trying to save anyone. Now I know why Mandy kept quiet about you. I don't think I'm helping you and this is not helping me.

LYLA: What was it about Amanda that made you sleep with her?

HAL: God, I don't know. She was there, maybe. That's why. I did a lot of stupid things back then. Slept around a lot.

LYLA: What made you talk to her that night? What started it all?

HAL: I liked her smile. She asked me weird questions. Interesting ones. What do I see myself doing in five years? Ten years. Things like that. Things most women looking for one-night stands don't ask.

LYLA: What made you seek her out after ten years?

HAL: I told you I wanted to make amends for some things. I started getting these headaches about a year ago and they just got worse and worse. At first I thought I was working too hard or living too hard. Stress or guilt even—

> *LYLA starts to move toward HAL, he steps back to retreat, but instead, LYLA moves over to the pile of utensils, grabs one of the weirder looking items then moves to her orbital module.*

LYLA: Could you hand me more duct tape? This thing has got to be ready for its test tomorrow.

> *Confused more than ever, HAL hands her the duct tape.*

HAL: (*noticing something in the pile*) Are those airline peanuts? You must have a dozen packets or more.

LYLA: Shark repellent. In most test flights, the ocean is the safest place for landing. Astronauts are often provided with sufficient shark repellent just in case. Always be prepared.

HAL: Shark repellent, right. For the spaceship.

LYLA: Correct. I do wish I could take you with me. If I had known you'd be interested, I could have planned for this.

HAL: (*trying to find the most polite of exit strategies*) Yeah, OK. Look, good luck with your "flight."

LYLA: Amanda was the first one you sought out. The only one you've been looking for.

HAL: Maybe. Yeah. I never forgave myself for her.

LYLA: If you want to keep lying to yourself, don't let me stop you.

HAL: What do you know? You're just some crazy, perverted sister she kept hidden away from the world. If I hadn't stumbled upon you, no one would know you existed.

LYLA: She didn't keep me hidden! I came here of my own free will. I needed to think. And you don't have a lot of time.

HAL: (*overly defensive, as if she's touched on something*)   What do you mean by that? What do you know? You needed a place to think, right. Because you can't build a rocket ship in your backyard, the neighbors may talk. OK, look, I never thought I had anything to apologize for, with her, that week, that night, but when I look back over the last few decades, only a few things stick with me and Mandy's conversations were one of them.

> *LYLA rips off a strip of duct tape and covers Hal's mouth then returns to her work.*

LYLA: Words tend to shoot out of you like propulsion. You shouldn't waste that energy. How did you imagine this would go, Hal? Get a number, give her a call, talk for a few hours then things would just work themselves out? Instead, you are on the brink of something glorious. Something so few have experienced. You want to find Amanda? Come with me. You're cute, confused, even when you are wasting propulsion feeling sorry for yourself. I've just decided I need a copilot. A few adjustments over the next few days, weight ratio adjustments, another seat, some steering, and welcome aboard.

HAL: (*removing the duct tape slowly*)   I don't think so. (*joking*)   I wouldn't pass the physical. The headaches, well, they weren't stress induced. With how I was living, I always thought I'd get a venereal disease, never a brain tumor.

LYLA: Looking for a cure turned into looking for a savior. Time to start making new memories, Hal. And since I know the pilot and the engineer, I think I can pull a few strings. Mandy was your last stop? Last chance? No. But it may be a hell of a way to find out what's next. Hand me the . . .

HAL: Yeah, I know. Duct tape.

LYLA: Did you know that zero gravity may have all kinds of odd effects on the human body—slowing bodily functions, distorting them? Scientists even theorize living in space will change our body chemistry, extending life, changing our immune systems, even slowing tumor growth and degenerative neurological disorders.

> *After a pause but without a word, HAL grabs a leaf, eats it, picks up the duct tape, and sits by her as they work together.*

> *BLACKOUT. END OF PLAY.*

Problems

Sometimes the best experience a theatre artist can get is working on new, very raw, unfinished, even bad, material. The following group of plays are broken, incomplete. Plays in need of help. The plays have interesting setups that experiment with offstage action, strange dialogue, odd property, and odd worlds. Often, the plays feel unfinished. Two of the plays have a single similar line, another product of a writing process. These plays have flaws, but they also have a lot of potential for creativity and playfulness. Some of the plays include verbal "stunts" where the characters must make quick shifts in tone or intention, toying with the audience's expectations.

❧ Stuffed Animals ❧

Two people: flexible casting; single set.

Two minimum wagers entertain themselves on a slow day at their mall job but what exactly are they selling and what is the cost?

Page-to-Stage Challenges:
- Very simple setup with lots of potential staging flexibility
- Odd dialogue with disturbing implications
- Power dynamics
- Worldbuilding and what's unseen

Questions to Ponder/Answers to Seek:
- How do the characters' relationships and power dynamics shift as the play goes along?
- What visual elements are necessary to tell the story and which elements are not?
- How does the offstage action affect the characters?
- What is real and what is metaphor in this story?

Stuffed Animals

a transaction

Characters:

Kelly   Slacker, runs the register.

Dobra   Slacker, runs the rest.

Setting   The front interior entrance of Fluffies, a small toy store in a burned-out, dying strip mall.

> KELLY is at a register looking out, scanning the mall, in a focused search for something elusive. DOBRA walks in, sees KELLY scanning, and joins in. A few moments pass as we see both move their glances left and right, slowly but with precision. They continue to scan the random passersby as they talk.

KELLY: Nope.

DOBRA: Not that one.

KELLY: That?— Uh-uh.

DOBRA: Here we go. She coming this way? I think we got one. And . . . nope. Going into Shirts Galore.

KELLY: Not getting a lot of nibbles today.

DOBRA: Yeah, two early this morning. That's been it. Thought today was going to be a good one.

KELLY: This isn't good. Not good at all. We have quotas, Tony says. Do I have to remind you? "Quotas, Kelly. Quotas, Dobra!"

DOBRA: We have quotas. Who doesn't understand that? I understand we have quotas. He was very clear.

KELLY: Very clear. And very scary.

> DOBRA roars weirdly.

KELLY: (*pause as the sound echoes and dies*)   I'm starving. What time is it?

DOBRA: You just got off break thirty minutes ago.

KELLY: Dobra, what about him? That guy. Coming out of the Chicken Shack?

DOBRA: He won't even look this way.

KELLY: Bet me? Five bucks says he makes eye contact.

DOBRA: Eye contact? Is that what we've stooped to? Eye contact? I'm not betting on eye contact. Tony doesn't want eye contact. He wants bodies . . . in the store. They have to enter the store. Five bucks.

KELLY: Forget it.

DOBRA: If you can get him to a back aisle, ten bucks.

KELLY thinks about the offer.

KELLY: If I get him into the stockroom, twenty.

DOBRA: Fine. I'm bored . . . and a little hungry too. Ten dollars if you get him to the back of the store. If you get him into inventory, I'll also give you a fifteen-minute break. Because you're hungry.

KELLY: Deal.

DOBRA: OK, Kelly, you're up. Let's see you work your magic.

KELLY moves out from behind the register, grabs a register microphone (or bullhorn) and moves closer to the entrance. The following monologue starts so gleefully and with such joy but slowly devolves into anger and madness as we watch KELLY fail to lure the customer over.

KELLY: Hey, everyone! Sales! Sales! Sales! Lots of inventory! Low, low prices! You need something? We got it! Your kid needs a teddy bear? We got it! Birthday gifts? We got them! Fluffies has it all! Fluffy Bear and all his friends! Jenny the Guinea Hen! Topher Turtle and Cattle-lina the Amooo- zing Cow! Garth the Gap-Toothed Gargoyle! And let's not forget His High Holiness Pope Platypus the Second! We have everything you can dream of at Fluffies!!! Fluffies! We make dreams come true! WE MAKE DREAMS COME TRUE! DREAMS! We have dreams here! Dreams here, people!!! Dreams . . . eff.

DOBRA:	(*their eyes follow the customer moving on past the store*) As he walks past Fluffies to Del Burger Vista.
KELLY:	(*grabbing a stuffed animal from a display*) I'm going to rip this thing's head off.
DOBRA:	Woah! Inventory! That's not like you. Hangry?
KELLY:	YES! I haven't eaten since this morning.
DOBRA:	The day's not over. Any moment now could be a wellspring. Suddenly, there'll be lines out the door. Aisles bursting. All shapes and sizes. Ripe for the picking. Tony's not here so no boss breathing down our necks. Yes, we have quotas. Don't remind me but for now, we are the lions. We rule the kingdom. We can do whatever we want! And it's all ours! They're all ours! Every stinking one of them! Right fricking here! Fluffies's Stuffies Emporium is all freaking ours!!!

> *DOBRA pulls out something wrapped in white paper. KELLY stares blankly at him.*

DOBRA:	(*continued*) I made a few sandwiches with leftovers.
KELLY:	Dobra! You are a lifesaver! This smells delicious.
DOBRA:	What can I say? I'm a master chef.
KELLY:	Pride goeth before the fall.
DOBRA:	My braggadocio is in check.
KELLY:	Not a word.
DOBRA:	Yes, it is! Braggadocio is definitely a word.
KELLY:	We'll agree to disagree. (*beat*) Can I eat it now?
DOBRA:	(*leaving well enough alone*) I'm not sure I want people walking in and seeing you eating at the register. What would Tony say?
KELLY:	I'll take it back down the aisle. Near the Barbies. Or the old wooden toys. No one goes down that aisle. Who wants a waddling wooden duck anymore? Or a rocket ship you drag around on a string? I'll eat it near the yo-yo display! That place is a wasteland.

DOBRA: (*sighing*)   Just . . . eat it here. But eat it fast and keep it covered up in case someone walks by.

KELLY: Done. Thank you, Dobra.

> *KELLY unwraps the sandwich and takes a huge bite then another, ravenously. KELLY destroys the sandwich.*

KELLY: (*woozy from the food orgasm*)   Oh, man. Sleepy.

DOBRA: Too fast. You ate it too fast.

> *KELLY begins to pick at their teeth, then sucks them as if gathering every morsel.*

KELLY: I owe you one. Big time. If I have to walk out there, club someone over the head, and drag them into Pope Platypus the Second's confessional, then that's where I am with what you just did for me.

DOBRA: No, Kelly. Where's the sport in that? Any one of these places could just leap on some rando, yank them into their establishment, sell the mindless sheep something they don't want, and push them right back out into the street. What we do takes a little more finesse.

KELLY: We work in a mall.

DOBRA: Is that what you see? Is that what you think we're doing here? Is that why you do this every day? No day off?

KELLY: You don't take days off either.

DOBRA: We have our nights. I can live with that arrangement.

KELLY: There's got to be more to living than just playing spider and fly all day long. Ya know, the big cats hunt and stalk their prey. Pack animals use their wits to chase things down relentlessly until what they want collapses, exhausted and helpless. We're stuck. Our territory stops at the door. Right at this line. And out there is open land. From Pretty Pretty Bang Bang Boutique to Pantsappalooza! From the Tacopocalypse to Carpets Carpets Carpets! We just sit and wait.

DOBRA: That's why we work for minimum wage.

KELLY: Minimum wage!

DOBRA: (*apparently changing the subject*) Would you rather have too much to eat or not enough?

KELLY: Well, that's easy. Too much. Who wants to starve?

DOBRA: Yes, but to the those who have too much do they really know what they have? And to the starving, a fly could be a feast.

KELLY: I don't know where to put that information. It's not filling. It's not satisfying a craving.

DOBRA: Did you hear about Angela? Gone.

KELLY: Wait. What? Angela. That tall gazelle that Tony chased around? Gone?

DOBRA: Vanished last week. They broke up. She left the house, said she was going for a walk. Then . . . disappeared.

KELLY: I don't believe you. She's just hiding out or found herself a new herd. She's out there somewhere. It's just a matter of time before she turns up. She'll get thirsty or hungry, will need to stop and feed. That's when ol' Tony or some other thickskulled killing machine will leap out of the water or a bush and grab her by the neck and then, only then, will she be gone. She's a victim. And all those other gazelles will just run off and watch her get dragged under the surface.

DOBRA: I feel bad for her. Tony? Not a nice guy. I mean, he's the boss. But . . .

KELLY: Hey, it's eat or be eaten.

DOBRA: I know. I know. But still if things were different . . . if the world were different . . .

KELLY: You getting soft?

DOBRA: No. Just philosophical.

KELLY: Same thing. (*sighs*) I may be watching too many nature documentaries.

DOBRA: I have to lay off the PBS.

KELLY: What if that's it? What if one day this place is empty? No
              one. No Tony even. We look out over once prosperous,
              lush fields to nothingness. What then?

DOBRA: That is something to be considered.

              KELLY looks at their own arm and sniffs it, licks it
              slightly. KELLY shudders at the thought.

DOBRA: (*an idea*) You could be the new Tony. I could be the
              new Tony. We would run things.

KELLY: But without food?

DOBRA: Yeah, we would need food.

KELLY: Without an income? Without any way to sustain
              ourselves?

DOBRA: Oblivion is an empty stomach.

              A pause.

KELLY: So let's pretend the next meatball saunters into the
              store.

DOBRA: I'm listening.

KELLY: Just walks in like they own the place. Not a care in the
              world. Relaxed. Full of nonchalantness.

DOBRA: Not a word but I'm following.

KELLY: And we lead Mr. or Ms. Not-A-Care all around the
              place. Show off the merchandise. Make them feel really
              at home. We bathe them in attention. Yes, ma'am.
              Of course, sir. We have exactly what you need right
              over here, monsieur, or whatever, and all the titles
              and words that go with a good show. I mean we have
              them really defenseless. They suspect nothing. Right
              at that moment, when they're about to make all of our
              dreams come true, BAM! Shotgun to the face! They
              turn the tables on us. I mean you're bleeding out of
              your face hole. I'm screaming as BLAM! A shot to
              my gut! DOBRA! NOOOOOO! I see your body fall.
              I'm bleeding out. This seemingly unaware rodent has
              claws! Well, not claws! A shotgun.

DOBRA:	And we didn't notice the shotgun when they entered the store?
KELLY:	For the purposes of this story, no, we did not.
DOBRA:	Go on. I'm intrigued.
KELLY:	No, that's it.
DOBRA:	That's it? That's nothing. That's terrible. You're saying all we do and dream of is for naught?
KELLY:	We dream a lot, Dobra. I'm tired of just dreaming. We talk big. I'm tired of just talking.
DOBRA:	So you suggest . . . keep in mind, Tony.
KELLY:	Tony promises big things. Well, not so much promises as threatens us if we don't meet our quotas.
DOBRA:	But Tony isn't here. Tony doesn't call the shots at this particular moment. We do.
KELLY:	We do! Yeah.

KELLY scans the mall, possibly searching for prey.

DOBRA:	We are dealing with small potatoes when we should be thinking of dealing with our here and now. We're always thinking about today when we should be thinking about tomorrow.
KELLY:	Yeah, Thursday.
DOBRA:	No, not Thursday. Figurative. The future. We should be thinking of what's standing in the way of our future. Tony.
KELLY:	We should do something about Tony. What should we do about Tony?
DOBRA:	We should . . . get rid of Tony.
KELLY:	Totally. We should report Tony to the owner.
DOBRA:	Yeah. No. Report Tony to the owner? What does that do? You think the owner is going to listen to us? We're hunter-gatherers. Not fat cats. We can't just stroll in and "report Tony." We'll be his next meal.

KELLY:	Right. (*an idea*) We should get rid of Tony. Yeah, we should take out Tony. Then we run things. We get all the spoils. The land—this mall—and all it contains becomes ours!
DOBRA:	Now you're talking big leagues, Kelly. We're not joking around here. Now you're thinking like a king of the jungle!
KELLY:	I knew you watched those nature shows!
DOBRA:	I may have watched a few.
KELLY:	He won't know what hit him. (*a realization*) Maybe he doesn't come in today.
DOBRA:	Maybe.

They both sigh simultaneously as life passes by.

KELLY:	Survival on minimum wage!
DOBRA:	Minimum wage!
KELLY:	(*almost singing it*) MINIMUM WAGE!
DOBRA:	We should check on our inventory. What if, what if, what if, am I right?
KELLY:	Yeah. Right. We need to make sure we're good . . . for now.
DOBRA:	After you.
KELLY:	Thank you. You're my best friend, Dobra.
DOBRA:	Thanks, buddy. And you are mine.

KELLY exits toward the back of the store, smiling. DOBRA reaches under the counter and pulls out a creepy, scarred and very worn baseball bat, throws it over their shoulder and exits with a smile, following KELLY.

BLACKOUT. END OF PLAY.

❧ Holly and Jesus ❧

Two people: one female, one flexible; a simple set.

Holly really needs this Easter pageant to go smoothly. She never thought the problem would come from a savior who is ready to shake things up.

Page-to-Stage Challenges:
- Very few stage directions
- Very flexible staging
- The final Jesus monologue
- Offstage versus onstage action

Questions to Ponder/Answers to Seek:
- How do the relationships between the two characters shift as the story progresses?
- How does the urgency of the situation and between the characters intensify or expand as the story progresses?
- What are the apparent and not-so-apparent struggles of each character?

Holly and Jesus
a revival

Characters:

Holly   She has an Easter pageant to put on.

Jesus   He has issues.

Setting   The sanctuary of a large church. Decorations, possibly
           livestock abound.

> *The lectern and nave of a church sanctuary, decorated
> for an Easter pageant. White cloth and flowers
> everywhere. Up center stage there is a magnificent
> cross that towers over everything else. HOLLY enters.*

HOLLY: (*calling*)   JESUS!

> *There is no answer.*

HOLLY: (*calling*)   JESUS! Where are you?!

> *After another beat of silence, suddenly, JESUS enters,
> clothed in white robes, beard, crown, etc. He saunters
> in, very confused.*

HOLLY: Where have you been? Everyone one else is ready.

JESUS: I have a few questions.

HOLLY: Really? You have questions? We're going to open
           the doors soon. You can't imagine how many people
           showed up. It's our biggest day. The Virgin Mary is
           ready. The prostitute. What's her name.

JESUS: Her name is also Mary. Magdalene.

HOLLY: Yeah, we got her as well. All of the apostles.

JESUS: Disciples.

HOLLY: What's the difference? Disciples. Apostles.

JESUS: There's a difference. I'm just saying.

HOLLY: We really are going to need you on that cross in . . .
           (*checks watch*)   holy crap.

JESUS: I'm really not . . .

HOLLY: Feeling it? Jesus, we don't have time for a crisis right
            now.

JESUS: It's not that. I just am wondering . . . I mean I'm up
            there . . . and they, the people, are down here.

HOLLY: (*trying to hurry him along*)   In the sanctuary.

JESUS: Yes. So I'm up there and they are down here . . .

HOLLY: And we have the two Marys and the disciples.

JESUS: Yes, and all the decoration. I'm just thinking that it may
            be a bit much.

HOLLY: This is an Easter pageant. Much is literally what it's
            about. What part of pageant are you not familiar with?

JESUS: No. I mean . . . shouldn't it be a more somber event?

HOLLY: I don't write this stuff. It's in the manual.

            HOLLY holds up a Bible.

JESUS: Where's the tomb? With the stone rolled away—

HOLLY: (*trying to move things along, looking offstage*)   It's
            offstage. . . . Over there somewhere. Mary! No. The
            other one. So when we get Jesus up there on that cross,
            the music will play, the lights will go down, and you
            will enter . . . weeping. Can we do that? Good.

JESUS: I know this is a big deal.

HOLLY: The biggest. I really need you in place, man.

JESUS: Yes, I'm getting there. Just a minute. What if we do it a
            little differently this time?

HOLLY: Differently? What differently? We do it like we've
            always done it. How else would we do it? You on the
            cross. The "skies" grow dark. A lot of weeping and
            wailing. Then there's the tomb, the stone rolls away.
            Bright light. You appear. Rejoicing. Everyone goes
            home. See you next year.

JESUS: But is that the best we can do? I'm thinking this time we
            try something different. Maybe people will respond . . .
            differently. Better.

HOLLY:	Better? There is no better. You get crucified. You die. You rise from the dead. And everyone believes in you. Worships God. Everyone's happy.
JESUS:	But are they? We've been doing this for how long now? A couple of millennia, right? And sure, for a week or two, maybe a month, people treat each other well. They're relatively content. Less worried. At peace. But sooner or later, they forget. Until we do this whole show again same time, next year. If you ask me, we're wasting a lot of time and resources for a quick little, "Oh, yeah, that's what it's all about."
HOLLY:	You're joking, right? Who put you up to this? Gary? Lynn? Was it Lynn? It was Lynn, wasn't it? She's had it out for my job ever since I wouldn't let her be a wise man.
JESUS:	It wasn't Lynn. It wasn't Gary. I just think we should consider how we use the time we have. Maybe freshen this up. No one is really moved by the whole crucifixion thing any more. They see the pictures on everything. On jewelry. Paintings. It's even on that window. (*he points*) I don't think we should do it like this anymore.
HOLLY:	You're going to ruin this for me. Weeks I've been planning and coordinating. Phone calls, scheduling. An animal handler. I got camels. I got a donkey. A well-mannered donkey. Not like that demon we had last year that took a bite out of the Roman centurion. A really nice donkey. His name is Odie. Donkey Odie. He's adorable.
JESUS:	You're very good at your job.
HOLLY:	Everything is ready. I've got the entire ensemble waiting on a cue from me as soon as I get you up there on that cross.
JESUS:	So I get on that cross, we run the whole thing, and then what?
HOLLY:	We all get paid and we go home.

JESUS: I just think if I had a little leeway to change one or two things, if you allowed me a little liberty to go off script, I think you'd like what you'd see. And better yet, those people out there would witness something that resonates, really sticks with them. I mean something that they will never forget.

HOLLY: Look . . . dude . . . Jesus.

JESUS just stares at HOLLY with doe eyes.

HOLLY: What do you have in mind?

JESUS: OK. Thank you. Thank you. Thank you. You will not be disappointed. I have some really great ideas.

HOLLY: Yes. Yes, I'm sure. What ideas?

JESUS: Well, anything's on the table really. But what I was thinking, what if instead of going up on that cross, I grab the first person I see and just give them a big hug?

HOLLY stares, speechless.

JESUS: I mean a really big hug. A bear hug. Lift them off their feet, spin them around in my big bear hug. Really give it to them. Then—

HOLLY: Get up on the cross.

JESUS: Here me out.

HOLLY: A hug?! That's what they are going to remember? A hug?

JESUS: Well, now hold on. I don't have to stop with just one hug. I can move to the next person. Grab Mary Magdalene. Hug her too.

HOLLY: On the cross please.

JESUS: OK, so not all of the ideas are home runs. And that's a no on the bear hug. What about—

HOLLY: Do you have any "ideas" that end with you on that cross?

JESUS: Well, no. . . . I thought I would steer away from that image. Like I said, it feels stale. I just don't think anyone really gets it anymore. Sure, it's a powerful image. Or it was. But been there, done that, right? What those people need is something immediate, something they can empathize with. No one's been crucified in a thousand years. Maybe two. Maybe I should get shot? With a whole drawn out death scene. I could say a few lines of scripture, "Forgive them for they know not what they do." Yada yada yada. You know, the big ones that everyone expects.

HOLLY: Yada yada? There were no guns in first century Jerusalem. How would you be shot? Get on the freaking cross, man. I don't have time for some crisis. I need a savior on that cross!

JESUS: I think we're really missing a golden opportunity here. And I think it's important to give the people what they pay for. And I think you're not even giving this a chance. Look, being crucified wasn't anything special back then anyway. The Romans crucified everybody. They doled out crosses like candy. And I wasn't the last. They kept doing it long after me.

HOLLY: It's what the people expect. It's in the book.

JESUS: Well, maybe, as I am Jesus, I'm not supposed to be what they expect. Maybe I'm supposed to surprise them. Maybe they come in here thinking they are seeing a crucifixion and I give them—TADA!— something else.

HOLLY: I'm not sure that's what they want. You start messing with their expectations and we're all going down. You and I are out of a job. Or worse. Children's theatre. Let me ask you. What are the Marys going to do? The disciples? You think Peter and Andrew are really fishermen? We're in Iowa.

JESUS: I'm just asking for one chance. One time to try something a little different. If I see it's not working, I'll ad-lib a bit and get us back to what we were planning originally.

HOLLY: I can't believe I'm going to . . .

JESUS: YES! You won't be disappointed. And if you are or the crowd just aren't feeling it, blame it on me. I'm Jesus, right? How mad can you get at Jesus?

HOLLY: If you start changing things, they won't see Jesus anymore. They're going to lose their minds.

            JESUS is deep in thought, pacing, silently brainstorming.

HOLLY: Are you ready?

JESUS: Not yet.

HOLLY: (*after a long beat*)   I'm going to need something. I have to cue the Marys, the Roman guards, the disciples . . .

JESUS: OK, OK. I think I'm ready. Open the doors!

HOLLY: And what is my cue?

JESUS: Believe me, you'll know. You have nothing to worry about. This is going to be something to remember.

HOLLY: Whatever. I'm tired. I'm letting them in. We go on your cue.

            JESUS gives her a thumbs up. HOLLY exits. There is a long pause. We hear the sound of doors opening and the buzz of a crowd filling the sanctuary, maybe an "ooh" or an "aah" at the stage decorations.

JESUS: Come in, brothers and sisters, rejoice and be glad. For today is a special day.

            The buzz of the crowd dies down. JESUS scans the crowd with a warm, welcoming smile. After a few beats, there is an expectation but nothing happens. JESUS continues to stare out at the crowd. Nothing. Is JESUS experiencing stage fright? After another few awkward moments, JESUS speaks.

JESUS: An impression.

            JESUS cups his hands to his mouth but then forgets that he left out a step.

JESUS: The Holy Spirit.

          JESUS returns his hands to his mouth and he makes the sound of flapping wings. Silence.

JESUS: (*not to be deterred*)   What did Dorothy say to the Pope?

          Silence.

JESUS: There's no place like Rome.

          More silence.

JESUS: That's a Wizard of Oz joke. Any Wizard of Oz fans here today?

          Silence.

JESUS: OK, this isn't what you expected. I'm not a comedian. I'll leave the jokes to the Franciscans. Am I right?

HOLLY: (*from offstage somewhere, just audible*)   Oh, dear Lord.

JESUS: I heard that. Look, I know I'm not what you were expecting. You came here for a crucifixion. And I could give you that, but then you wouldn't get this! Could I get the lights lowered a bit please?

          The lights do not change. JESUS then appears to make a shadow puppet in the form of a bird and makes it "fly" around the space. Once again, there is a deafening silence.

HOLLY: (*from offstage*)   Back on the cross, Jesus.

JESUS: No, wait. So you'd rather have this?!

          Starting from one end of the front row and continuing on through the audience, JESUS begins pointing to each person.

JESUS: (*continued*) Sinner. Sinner. Sinner. Sinner. Sinner. Sinner. Possible saint, but mostly a sinner. Sinner. Sinner. Sinner. Sinner. BIG Sinner. Sinner. Sinner. Sinner. Don't even try to fool me, Sinner. Sinner. GIGANTIC Sinner! HUGE. Still a sinner. You're a sinner. You're a sinner. And you. You. You. You. Yes, you too. Stop looking at me like that, sinner. You're a big sinner. Sinner. Sinner. Sinner. Annnnnnnnd SINNER! Does that get everyone? Good. Feel better? Want to help your fellow man now? No, you don't, do you? You feel lousy! And you should. But I don't want you to feel lousy. I want you to . . . learn to juggle. (*changing his mind*) No, I want you to . . . (*racking his brain*) To . . . to . . . to enjoy this dinner we've prepared for you right outside those doors you just entered. If you turn right around and walk right back outside, a HUGE banquet awaits you. Come on. Up. Get up. Everyone up! Up! Up! Turn around and make your way out those doors. Sing with me as you do. (*singing, possibly clapping*)

>   He's got the whole world . . . in His hands. He's got the whole world . . . in his Hands. He's got the whole world . . . in his Hands. He's got the whole world in his Hands.

>   *A buzz of the crowd exiting in confusion is heard. HOLLY enters. She is incredibly angry.*

HOLLY: There is no food out there, is there?

JESUS: Maybe there is. Maybe there isn't.

HOLLY: But there isn't, is there?

JESUS: No.

HOLLY: I wish I could crucify you.

JESUS: Crisis builds faith, Holly. Chaos breeds faith, Holly. When they walk out into that very empty hallway, they will find nothing. They will seek answers. Probably from us.

HOLLY: But we'll be long gone.

JESUS: We'll be long gone. Out the back door. Hopefully there is one. They will have to find the answers on their own. And if there is a God, they will find him. A miracle!

HOLLY: I hate pageants.

JESUS: I do too. But I love a good mystery. And that, my dear Holly, is what makes it all worthwhile. It's not the cross. It's the third day. It's the empty tomb. Every good story needs a mystery to solve. It's the heart of everything. Science, philosophy, religion. The movie Who Framed Roger Rabbit? It's all about the mystery.

HOLLY: That's a really old reference. OK, I have a mystery for you. When are we getting paid?

JESUS: Maybe we already have.

HOLLY: No. We haven't.

They exit. We hear the crowd noise start to rise a bit out of confusion or anger.

BLACKOUT. END OF PLAY.

☙ Big Head ☙

Two roles: two males, but can be flexible; simple set.

Two siblings face off after a family fight at dinner that will determine how one chooses to live their life from this point forward.

Page-to-Stage Challenges:
- Very few stage directions
- Sibling relationships
- Unseen characters
- Odd props
- Generational politics
- Identity politics
- Peer pressure

Questions to Ponder/Answers to Seek:
- How does the siblings' relationship enter into play with this story?
- How do the unseen parents affect the story?
- What are the underlying struggles of the characters?

Big Head

a grandstand

Characters:

Neil   High school junior, small, normally he'd go unnoticed, but not today.

Blake   Neil's older brother, athletic.

Setting   A bedroom. A closet door. A door that keeps Dad at bay.

PRODUCTION NOTE: Feel free to change the ways that the characters refer to the headpiece based on the costume props used. For example, instead of referring to it as a rabbit head, it could be a badger, armadillo, etc. It doesn't matter what the fluffy head costume piece looks like, just that the head looks really over-the-top silly.

> *A bedroom. Two brothers. NEIL is fuming. BLAKE is trying to play peacemaker.*

BLAKE: You were in the wrong.

> *NEIL doesn't respond immediately. He's brooding.*

BLAKE: (*continued*)   You were in the wrong. And you know it.

NEIL: (*just reacting*)   No, you were wrong.

BLAKE: I was wrong?! How was I wrong?

NEIL: I don't know. I just need someone to be wrong at this moment. (*beat*)   I just want to be able to have a simple conversation with him. That's all. Is that too much to ask? Civilized conversation? I'm a freaking junior in high school. I have thoughts. I have my own opinions on things.

BLAKE: On the game. On school. On music. On the country. On the president.

NEIL: Just like everyone else. I have a lot of thoughts. Why can't I just share them with him without it becoming a thing?

BLAKE: Right. That's all you were doing. Just trying to share. Not trying to start something.

NEIL: I was not trying to start anything.

             A beat.

BLAKE: He's our dad. He knows a lot, Neil. You're just a smart-ass. That's your problem.

NEIL: You idolize him. That's yours.

BLAKE: It's the same every time. He says something and you're triggered. You just have to say something back. To prove how smart you are.

NEIL: It was important this time. He needs to know that I don't think like he does. That I am not going to stand by and let that go. Just let what he says linger on out there like we all agree with him.

BLAKE: Well, now you don't have your car for a week.

NEIL: And I have you in here pestering me. Every time. It always comes to this. "Go to your room." I'm seventeen. For Christ's sake.

BLAKE: I think it may have been the f-bomb that really sent you here.

NEIL: What else was I to do?

BLAKE: Not say the f-bomb.

NEIL: I get really frustrated. We talk and talk and I run out of patience.

BLAKE: He knows that if he can just keep at you, he can beat you down.

NEIL: He thinks I'm an idiot. Like I couldn't possibly know how the world works. He actually said that. "You're so naïve." In a year it won't matter. I'll be gone. I'm going to go as far away from here as I possibly can. I don't care if it's BFE Community State, I am out of here.

BLAKE: So you finally told him. That should at least make you feel a bit of relief.

NEIL: It doesn't though. I feel worse now than before. That's the worst part. It was my secret. Like something I owned. No one else. Now he knows. Mom knows. You know.

BLAKE: Well, I've known for a while.

NEIL: Thank you, by the way. For keeping it on the down low.

BLAKE: That's what I'm here for. You need a conspirator.

NEIL: It's not like it's abnormal.

BLAKE: For him it is. He's from a different generation.

NEIL: That's no excuse. If you were only born in the fifties you don't get to excuse "Whites Only" signs.

BLAKE: Dad was born in the eighties.

NEIL: I know. I was trying to be—

BLAKE: A smart-ass.

NEIL: No.

BLAKE: Dad's not racist.

NEIL: Yeah, well, the group he runs with is.

BLAKE: I don't think Dad "runs" with a group. I don't think he's "run" with a group for a long time.

NEIL: You know what I mean.

BLAKE: And all of this because of the . . . thing.

NEIL: I didn't show him that. And it's not a thing.

BLAKE: Whatever it is. Where is it?

> *After a brief moment, NEIL goes to his closet and pulls out a large furry head like what might belong to a full-sized cartoon animal costume and sets in on his bed with the mask and its big, goofy smile staring out into the audience.*

BLAKE: (*continued*)   It's going to take him some time.

NEIL: He will never accept it. It's weird I know.

BLAKE: Weird? Let's say it's going to take some getting used to.

NEIL: Don't sugar coat it. He thinks I'm a freak. He doesn't understand. He never will. He accepts you. Why not give me this?

BLAKE: Well, I'm the athlete. Every family has to have one athlete.

NEIL: What does that make me?

             BLAKE points at the fuzzy head.

NEIL: He will never understand.

BLAKE: You're probably right. Do you have the rest of it?

NEIL: Yes. It's in the closet.

BLAKE: For this not to feel like an after-school special, hiding it in the closet was a terrible idea.

NEIL: It's too big to fit under my bed. What else was I going to do? I'm just going to put it on and go out there. Then he'll have to face me. He'll be confronted by his independent, open-minded, furry son.

BLAKE: And then you'll see a tear in his eye as the emotions of being so wrong all these years, after judging so many people, all the labels, all the innuendos, as he realizes that what he shunned and mocked all of these years was a part of him, his own son! His own furry son.

NEIL: At least it's not cake-sitting.

BLAKE: So what do you do in it?

NEIL: What's that supposed to mean?

BLAKE: I mean is it some weird sexual thing?

NEIL: What? No. You sound like dad. I just wear it.

BLAKE: All the time?

NEIL: (*frustrated, disappointed*) Well, not all the time. I'm comfortable in it.

BLAKE: And you think you're going to be able to go off to college wearing that all the time and have a normal life? Teachers going to call on you in class? "Hey, you, Mr. . . . you with the big furry head, what's the square root of this big number?"

NEIL: Maybe. Maybe college is different. More accepting of alternative lifestyles.

BLAKE:	Maybe. Or maybe it's worse. Even more exclusive cliques. More insecurity. More tribal instincts. More prone to attacking those that are different. More chance of that head ending up on a pike or worse. Dangling outside the window of some frat house.
NEIL:	I'm sure Mom and Dad in their heyday did all sorts of things they don't tell us. It was the '80s, right?
BLAKE:	I think Dad had an earring. If you look at his left ear, you can sort of see the indention where the hole was.
NEIL:	See, why doesn't he tell us that stuff? Shouldn't he be trying to prove he was or still is "cool." Trying to bond with us with stories from when he was our age. I mean I don't really want to hear them but isn't he supposed to be doing that?
BLAKE:	And him telling us about his earring or he and Mom doing weird stuff equates to your revelation about the giant rabbit head?
NEIL:	It's not a rabbit. And I need an ally here. Whose side are you on?
BLAKE:	In this unique little war, I'm Switzerland for now. I don't want to lose my car for a week.
NEIL:	Coward. Then why are you here?
BLAKE:	Where else do I have to go?
NEIL:	He just wants me to be more like you. Like him.
BLAKE:	So when did this become a thing?
NEIL:	It's not a thing. It's who I am.
BLAKE:	So when did you decide to figure out who you were?
NEIL:	After you won your last game. You tackled that guy and forced that fumble. You won the game. He was so proud. We waited for you at the restaurant to celebrate. There was one of the waiters or someone dressed in a big blue bunny costume greeting everyone who entered. We waited and waited. That stupid huge rabbit just staring me in the face. Silly expression. Just waving his giant furry paw at us.
BLAKE:	This is a Stephen King novel.

NEIL:	Weeks after, all I could think about was that stupid furry hand waving at me. That giant toothy grin burned into my brain. I went back to the restaurant and no big blue rabbit. A few days later, I walk past the dumpster. And what do I see? Staring out of a clear garbage bag? This outfit. It wasn't the big blue bunny but still. Who would throw something like that away?
BLAKE:	It probably takes up a lot of space.
NEIL:	I'm not going to throw this away. Or give it up.
BLAKE:	Wearing this to school would be a major mistake. I don't think they'd even allow you into a classroom.
NEIL:	Why? I'm just being me. It comforts me. I feel right in it. They should allow me that freedom. The freedom to be me.
BLAKE:	If someone is sitting behind you, they won't even be able to see the teacher or the board.
NEIL:	That's not my problem.
BLAKE:	Mom and dad aren't going to let you do it as things stand. What if you tell them it's a class assignment? Sort of like when the students have to take care of an egg or sack of flour all week? That doesn't solve the whole school thing but we're getting you out the door at least.
NEIL:	I've written this.

NEIL retrieves a note from a table or drawer and hands it to BLAKE.

BLAKE:	(*reading*) "My life has become a bitter pill that doesn't treat the symptoms from which I suffer." No, you can't give anyone this.
NEIL:	I made a stack. I was going to hand them out.
BLAKE:	It feels like you're either seeking attention or you're about to end it all.
NEIL:	Really? I didn't mean it like that. You see, I lack the words. It's the great lines that do it. The great writers. I lack the words. I lack . . .

BLAKE:	All sense of normalcy. This is going to get you killed by any number of low self-esteem meatheads that are having a bad day.
NEIL:	I lack profundity.
BLAKE:	Yeah, I don't know what that means. Right now, I sort of want to punch you. OK, as weird as this is, if you want to live your life in that, you have to convince me first. You're going to be really hot most of the time. It's over ninety most of the summer. Sweaty. How do you clean it? That will get expensive.
NEIL:	Stop trying to talk me out of this.
BLAKE:	I'm not. I just want you to realize the commitment. They may kick you out of the house. You want to wander the streets in that?
NEIL:	Maybe. Maybe I don't care.
BLAKE:	And do what? What are you going to do in that? Find a job?
NEIL:	Now you're really sounding like dad.
BLAKE:	I'm just trying to figure this all out. That's what he will do. Yes, his figuring it out will be bookended by a lot of yelling and arguing. But still, you want to do this? You have to think about all of it.
NEIL:	Why? Why can't I just be exactly who I want to be?
BLAKE:	Look, I can maybe keep half the team off of your back. A few of the mean girl groups. But that leaves a whole bunch of people just ready to chime in on the dude wearing the furry costume. Can you defend yourself? Are you ready?
NEIL:	Why must I defend myself?
BLAKE:	Because that's not the world. This isn't some really cool fantasy movie, Neil. It's weird. And as much as anyone might try and understand, it's still weird. Heck, I think it's weird but I'm on board. Because you're my brother and blood is thicker than . . . a big furry bunny head.
NEIL:	You're a good brother.
BLAKE:	They're going to laugh at me too.

NEIL: We can change the world one person at a time.

BLAKE: No, this isn't going to change people.

NEIL: You never know.

BLAKE: You're not that significant in the grand theme of things, Neil. We're not. We're just high schoolers.

NEIL: This changed you.

BLAKE: Caring about the physical welfare of my younger brother is not a change. I still don't get it. Neither will dad or mom.

NEIL: They don't have to get it. They just have to know it's me. Their son. Neil.

           NEIL picks up the head, puts it on and faces the door.

BLAKE: Neil the fuzzy.

           BLAKE tries his best to stand strong as he follows NEIL out the door to infinity and beyond.

           BLACKOUT. END OF PLAY.

❧ The Trapeze ❧

Two roles: flexible casting; a simple set.

Neville has bad news and instead of telling the love of his life, he has decided to flee. The brother of his love who happens to also love him must convince Neville that the coward's way out is not the best plan.

Page-to-Stage Challenges:
- A relatively straightforward play that allows for a wide array of staging options
- Line delivery and timing between two close friends
- Strange, uniquely personal, and even odd situations and choices
- The unseen third person just offstage
- A feeling of incompleteness at the end of the play

Questions to Ponder/Answer to Seek:
- How does what isn't said affect the relationship between the two characters?
- What role does urgency play in this particular scene?
- What questions need answering for the play to work? Which ones do not?
- How does mystery play in the telling of this story?
- What role does comedy play in this story?

The Trapeze

an escape

Characters:

Neville   Thin, nervous. Young. Can be between eighteen and early twenties. An overthinker for good reason.

Barker   Healthy-looking. Strong. Loyal. A little older than NEIL. Not the brightest.

Setting   A waiting place. A living area?

> *Two young men waiting. They occasionally stare at a door opposite, possibly out front toward the audience. One of the men, NEVILLE, is thin. The other, BARKER, is healthy-looking. NEVILLE is biting his nails. We hear the click-click of his teeth as he chews. Every few seconds or so he spits the work of his effort. BARKER tries to ignore him. Finally. . . .*

BARKER: Please stop.

> *NEVILLE continues. Click. Click. Spit.*

BARKER: Neville.

NEVILLE: I can't.

BARKER: You can. You are choosing not to.

NEVILLE: Easy for you to say. (*pause*)   It's the great lines that do it. The great writers. I don't have that. She'll never get it. She will never read between the lines. What the words aren't saying. (*pause*)   I don't think she's coming out.

BARKER: She's not been in there very long. (*checks his watch*)   Well, OK. It's been two hours. That's not good.

NEVILLE: That's not good at all. You think I left anything out? Like the why? I spent a lot of time retreading and bringing up the past.

BARKER: You mentioned the cat.

NEVILLE: I mentioned the cat. That's good, right?

> *BARKER is noncommittal.*

185

NEVILLE: She won't read between the lines. She won't get it.

BARKER: Then you'll try something else.

NEVILLE: I don't want to try something else. I'm done. I'm out.

BARKER: I know. I don't need the speech anymore. You've convinced me.

NEVILLE: I have?

BARKER: Well . . . enough to know I'm not going to change your mind. I don't like it but I guess I support the lunacy.

NEVILLE: It's not lunacy. It's a rational choice.

BARKER: OK, well, here. I bought you something. A little going-away present.

> *BARKER pulls a small wrapped item from his pocket. NEVILLE unwraps it to reveal . . .*

NEVILLE: A clown nose.

BARKER: I thought you might need it.

NEVILLE: I'm not going to become a clown. Trapeze artist. I want to become a trapeze artist.

BARKER: Oh. Sorry. In my head I still have this image of "running away to join a circus" thing. They still do the whole trapeze thing at a circus, right?

NEVILLE: (*referring back to the door*) She's never going to understand. I should have told her I was dying. I think I could have really done something with the whole life and death metaphor.

> *BARKER pulls a crumbled piece of paper from his other pocket, opens it and begins to read.*

NEVILLE: What's is that?

BARKER: Your first draft. (*reading*)   I think I like it better.

NEVILLE: Throw it away. I can't believe I asked for your advice.

BARKER: Look at it this way. You really had three choices. You could have told her that you were dying. That you were gay. Or that you were running away to join a circus. You chose the worst one.

NEVILLE: Dying isn't the worst one?

BARKER: Not even close.

NEVILLE: Profundity. I lack profundity.

BARKER: Yeah, I don't know what that means. (*referring back to the crumpled paper*)   You see, here you write, "My life has become a bitter pill that doesn't treat the symptom from which I suffer." That is heavy. Really heavy.

NEVILLE: And complete garbage.

BARKER: I should come with you.

NEVILLE: She's your sister. How's that going to work? I see you, I'm bound to see her.

BARKER: But I care about you too. Maybe more than she does. You don't even mention us.

NEVILLE: So you think I'm leaving because of you? Us?

BARKER: You're not? (*reading again*)   "The substance from which I am made and the pain I feel on a daily basis would ultimately cause you even more pain than you are in now." That is so . . . sacrificial. You are so noble in your selfishness.

NEVILLE: Wait. What?

BARKER: I said you're selfish, Neil. Self-consumed. A narcissist.

NEVILLE: No, read that again.

BARKER: "The substance from which I am made—"

NEVILLE: Oh, my God. That's not the first draft. They're mixed up. She has the wrong copy. I must have gotten them confused and gave her the wrong one.

BARKER: What's in the letter she has?

NEVILLE: It may be a few doodles and a really bad limerick about a man's genitals. I scratched out all of the good lines. She's going to think I'm insane.

BARKER: How many drafts did you write?

NEVILLE: Two or three. Dying, gay, and the circus thing.

BARKER: Trapeze.

NEVILLE: Yeah. That. There was one more where I confessed to being a serial killer.

BARKER: You are not good at this. Well, she's been in there a long time for a note with random scribblings on it. Maybe she thinks it's a joke. A really weird one.

NEVILLE: I'm going to knock on the door, go in, and just tell her.

BARKER: No, no. Bad idea. Let her come out. Think about what you're going to say to her. "Honey, I'm . . ."

   (struggling for the right words, they do not come)   You'll think of something.

NEVILLE: *(trying)*   Honey, I'm . . . joining the circus. And then her adorable little smile slowly fades to something more akin to a weird slash emoji.

BARKER: But you're not joining the circus.

NEVILLE: You know I'm not.

BARKER: And you and I?

NEVILLE: Aren't a thing. That's in your head.

BARKER: I'm in love with you.

NEVILLE: Yes, I know. You've mentioned it numerous times. You mentioned it the first time she introduced me to you. We laughed it off. Laughed and laughed. And laughed.

BARKER: I did a great job of hiding how much that hurt.

NEVILLE: Then she told me not to worry. Her brother falls in love with every one of her boyfriends.

BARKER: She knows me so well. Is that why you came to me first?

NEVILLE: I came to you because I trust you. I trust you almost as much as I trust her. That's why I told you, I confided in you. I thought, "I'll tell Barker first. Then I'll write a note to her."

BARKER: About joining the circus.

NEVILLE: No, trapeze artist. I thought maybe my weight loss could be explained with a training regimen. Trapeze artists are supposed to be thin. At least I've never seen a fat one. I even went so far as to build a small set of bars and a trapeze swing in my backyard to "practice."

BARKER: I'm not sure if that's more disturbing or attractive. But really this is about a breakup, right?

NEVILLE: I did have a physical. There was some irregular blood work.

BARKER: What?

NEVILLE: No. It's nothing. I just had a Kit Kat right before getting my blood drawn. I forgot about the eight hours without eating thing.

BARKER: So it could be nothing. How did we get to here?

NEVILLE: I may have heard the word "inoperable." I sort of tuned out. I was really hungry.

BARKER: You tuned out? The doctor was reviewing your blood tests and you tuned out?

NEVILLE: And here we are.

BARKER: You joining the circus. Possibly dying.

            NEVILLE sighs heavily then throws the clown nose at BARKER.

NEVILLE: Don't turn this into a thing about you.

BARKER: Oh, no. It's definitely about you.

NEVILLE: It's not about me.

BARKER: You aren't thinking of her, Nev. When you love someone, you want to be there. Through everything.

NEVILLE: Do you though? What if I don't want her to be there? I'd rather leave her angry at the person I was—whole, strong—then drag her into the horror show of watching me fall apart slowly over weeks.

BARKER: So one day you're just gone. Rather than spending the remaining time you have with her, you spend your time building a swing set in your backyard. Then you just leave. You don't even know if anything is wrong with you!

NEVILLE: Yes, but isn't there something wrong with a person who doesn't care to know if there is actually something wrong with him? And I did spend my time with her. I built the TRAPEZE during the day while she was working.

A moment of silence. Then NEVILLE goes back to biting his nails. Click. Click. Click.

BARKER: You know what? I'm not going to let you do this. That's my sister in there. You are the love of my life as unrequited as that may be. You're not leaving. She will come out in just a second and you will just . . . tell her.

NEVILLE: That I'm serial killer.

BARKER: No.

NEVILLE: That I'm gay.

BARKER: No.

NEVILLE: That I'm joining the—

BARKER: No, Nev!

NEVILLE: I will confess to knowing for some time that I am not fit for her. That fate had other plans. That the universe, God, mother nature, or L. Ron Hubbard had other plans for this body. For her. For me. For us. That what she thinks I am and what this body will do is wrong. I am a failed specimen. Our being together was an experiment gone wrong. That what she thought was . . . (*suddenly, an idea*)   I'll tell her I'm from another planet.

BARKER: Great idea.

BARKER does not believe it is a great idea.

NEVILLE: I'll tell her that my "species" gave me two years on this planet. That some choose to explore the world, some choose to eat everything in sight, some learn a new skill, some fall in love.

BARKER: That's genius.

BARKER does not believe it is genius.

NEVILLE: But now, my time is up. I must bid her adieu.

BARKER: Yes, say it like that. That is definitely going to work.

It will not work.

NEVILLE: That gives her two options. I'm insane, so it's lucky she found out now. Or she believes me and then I've completely overestimated her intelligence over the last two years. Either way, she'll say see you later, Neville! She's headed to college in a few months anyway. She'll eventually forget me and move on. Done.

BARKER: It's not the worst way to say goodbye. The best being actually saying goodbye. Giving her the chance to say goodbye to you.

NEVILLE: You're my best friend.

BARKER: No, don't say that. And I am not condoning this behavior. You're not dying. You're not gay. And you're not a serial killer.

NEVILLE challenges him with a look.

BARKER: (*continued*)   I'd know if you were a serial killer.

A pause.

BARKER: You heard every word the doctor said, didn't you?

NEVILLE doesn't answer.

BARKER: And this is the course of action you want to take? Trapeze artist.

NEVILLE: It's so outlandish and much better than reality.

BARKER: Well, I've written a note as well. Do you want to hear it?

NEVILLE: You can't tell her.

BARKER: You want to hear it?

> *NEVILLE doesn't answer so he reveals a note from his other pocket and reads.*

BARKER: (*reading*) Dear Sis, Nev is gone. He didn't join the circus. That was a lie but I'm hoping you knew that. Otherwise, I have to reevaluate our entire relationship. I may be the smart one and that's frightening. Neil's last words to me were of you—how much you meant to him, how much he will miss you. I'm not sure why he left. He seemed to have reasons that were too heavy for him to express. It is sudden. It is painful. It is a really crappy way to say goodbye. Let's face it. It's as bad as a goodbye as one could give. But maybe that's how things should be. Maybe bad goodbyes are exactly how all real goodbyes are supposed to be. Bad. They hurt. They are uncomfortable, even excruciating because they cost something. Or they should. Neil being gone cost him something too. He lost you.

NEVILLE: Why would you write this?

BARKER: Because I needed to say goodbye to you as well. And as bad as you think things are getting or how much you think your situation sucks, it's even worse for her and me. Because we'll be the leftovers. What remains. Go, be a trapeze artist, Neville. Or whatever.

> *NEVILLE exits.*

> *BLACKOUT. END OF PLAY.*

❦ Petunia Pulls Her Punch ❧

Two roles: both female, but flexible; a simple exterior.

Two garden enthusiast neighbors try to determine whether their meetings with the Antwerp Gardening Club are really what they believe them to be or if something more nefarious is going on in their world.

Page-to-Stage Challenges:
- Very few stage directions
- Flexible staging
- Vague references to an undefined or changing world
- Violent or disturbing implications in dialogue
- The juxtaposition of characters
- Potentially deceiving appearances

Questions to Ponder/Answers to Seek:
- What are the mysteries at play?
- What are the real needs of each character?
- How does the play shift in tone and world as the play progresses?

Petunia Pulls Her Punch

a dream

Characters:

Petunia Prim, proper and put together. She moves like a wood-land creature from a Disney film.

Tulip Her neighbor, the visual opposite of Petunia. Shocking, over-the-top, and all over the place, possibly pierced and heavily tattooed.

Setting A shared yard in front of a duplex.

> *Two doors divided by a small white fence. Walkways lead from each doorway to the sidewalk, separating the audience from a shared yard. In each yard is a flower bed. In one of the beds, we see a beautiful assortment of flowers, carefully tended, thriving. The other flower bed is struggling at best—the flowers are dull, drooping, one or two dead. After a moment, PETUNIA enters. She floats by, crossing up her walk toward her door. As she is about to enter the house, the door of the other abode opens. TULIP enters. She moves with a casual clumsiness.*

PETUNIA: You were missed.

TULIP: *(wishing she didn't have to respond)*   Oh, Petty dear.

PETUNIA: Tulip, please. You know I hate that.

TULIP: Fine. Petunia.

> *TULIP is about to exit back into her house when—*

PETUNIA: We missed you at the meeting.

> *TULIP begins to exit without acknowledging this comment but then stops and turns ready to engage.*

TULIP: I'm not going. I'm not ever going again.

PETUNIA: Oh.

TULIP: No. Never again.

PETUNIA: Well, that is a shame. You will be missed. You add such diversity to the conversations we have. You always provide a point of view missing from our regular agendas.

TULIP: (*incredulous*)   Right. Tell the ladies I said hello.

PETUNIA: Of course, of course. I hope your decision isn't because of something I've said.

TULIP starts to exit but once again stops and turns.

TULIP: What makes you say that?

PETUNIA: Or something I've done. It would really be very upsetting if I'd done something that in turn kept you away.

TULIP: No. It wasn't you. If it were, believe me, I'd enjoy telling you.

PETUNIA isn't convinced.

PETUNIA: Rest assured I won't be bringing my lemon meringue spritzer to any future meetings.

TULIP: Your punch. You think it's about your lemon punch? That's not—

PETUNIA: I'm just saying it's about tolerance. Inclusion. What one opens oneself up to. It's about sharing really. And it's a spritzer. Not a punch.

TULIP: Really? You really think the Antwerp Gardening Club will miss my particular point of view?

PETUNIA: No. They won't. They won't miss you at all. Just—Your flower bed really does need tending.

TULIP: They're fine.

PETUNIA: They're dying.

TULIP: I'm experimenting.

PETUNIA: With cruelty? Give those poor souls a drink. Some TLC would do wonders.

TULIP: I like the mise-en-scène that thorns and dead things set.

PETUNIA:	Of course, of course. And I am not one to interfere with our relationship. You're a pleasant neighbor.
TULIP:	Pleasant? I'll take it.
PETUNIA:	It's just—
TULIP:	I'm going inside now, Petunia.
PETUNIA:	Sure, sure. Just a moment more. I promise. It's just . . . I have been entertaining a rather wild notion that I cannot seem to shake. It has me a little, well . . . shaken. I need advice. From you. My neighbor.
TULIP:	From me? Advice? I say go for it.
PETUNIA:	You haven't heard the notion yet.
TULIP:	Look at me. Do I look like someone who weighs their decisions carefully?
PETUNIA:	That's not fair to you.
TULIP:	Those are your words. I'm literally quoting you.
PETUNIA:	Well . . . touché. (*beat*) I'm thinking of getting a tattoo.

TULIP laughs at the idea.

TULIP:	Is this one of your garden club jokes? I stop coming to your meeting so you ladies come up with this scheme to make fun of me and my ink?
PETUNIA:	No. NO! It's not a scheme. And I'm not the only one. I believe Rose may accompany me to the local tattoo parlor. She even mentioned a nose piercing. Quite scandalous. But she's very excited and I want to support her decision.
TULIP:	Well, that's grand. Great idea. The garden club will never be the same.
PETUNIA:	Yes. And I must say we owe it all to you.
TULIP:	Assimilation complete.
PETUNIA:	So what should I get?
TULIP:	Why suddenly ask me my opinion?

PETUNIA: Oh, come now. This isn't like you. Don't pout. You've never been one to avoid a topic. This is important to me, to us.

TULIP: No, you ladies, think that by getting a tattoo or piercing that all of a sudden you understand me? That you're broadening your horizons?

PETUNIA: That's not what I said at all. Now you're not being fair to us. We are trying. You're quite a foreign entity.

TULIP: I'm from Nebraska.

PETUNIA: That's not what I'm saying.

TULIP: You tell Rose, Lily, Jasmine, and the rest that I'm done with all of them.

PETUNIA: You don't enjoy our meetings, fine. I just thought it would be nice to have company, someone with whom I could go to these functions. They are so uncomfortable. Unbearable without my lemon spritzer.

TULIP: Then why go? Why submit to the weekly reminders?

PETUNIA: Sometimes just being near someone who may be in the same boat as you makes things seem just a bit better, easier. Makes the boat seem a little less lonely. You're angry. We're all angry.

TULIP: The talking isn't helping. They just keep it all fresh, staring at me. As if all of this even matters. As if all of this is actually here, real, tangible.

PETUNIA: The flowers are a nice touch.

TULIP: I really thought if I stopped watering them, they would just keep looking fresh and full, like they were made of plastic. The dying was a surprise. That sorta threw me for a loop.

PETUNIA: The accommodations are nice as well. They said we could rearrange things to our liking. Knock down walls, etc. Have the freedom, or at least the illusion of freedom. Well, that's something, right?

TULIP: I'm just tired, Petunia. Really tired.

PETUNIA: That's part of the protocol. The drugs do that. Everyone is trying their best to make us as comfortable as possible.

TULIP:	The fence? The sidewalk? The flowers? My clothes? Or are the drugs doing that too?
PETUNIA:	Who's to say?
TULIP:	Well, that is frightening.
PETUNIA:	It can be. Maybe it's all experimental. Maybe they don't even know what we're doing here. Like we're unmonitored. That doesn't seem right. (*excited by the idea*) Ooh, maybe we're guinea pigs.
TULIP:	And now it's worse.
PETUNIA:	Tulip, dear, the meetings—
TULIP:	Stop talking about the meetings! I'm not going back to the meetings!

> *PETUNIA is patient, quiet, allowing TULIP to vent. The indication is that TULIP is about to explode with emotion, but after a breath or two, she stifles herself, and says simply . . .*

TULIP:	(*continued*) A tattoo at this point in our lives seems so meaningless.
PETUNIA:	It might interest you to know that Lily is getting close. Another day or two maybe. We didn't think she was going to make it through the meeting we had and without you there the meeting was very short.
TULIP:	Yeah, that sucks. It is all going to suck. Large quantities of suck. Massive suck.
PETUNIA:	You know who lived in your place before you arrived?
TULIP:	Let me guess. Another flower?
PETUNIA:	Daisy. Daisy was here before I arrived. The first person I met. She invited me to the meetings. I never wanted to go either.
TULIP:	What? So Daisy dies and you take up the mantle?

> *PETUNIA nods softly in affirmation.*

TULIP:	(*continued*) You don't seem angry.
PETUNIA:	Yesterday I was.

TULIP:	You worked in your garden all day yesterday.
PETUNIA:	(*affirming*) While you blasted your death punk fusion records out your window. I'm not complaining. It's starting to grow on me especially that last song you played.
TULIP:	"Emilia's Bloody Hatchet"?
PETUNIA:	Yes. I like that song a lot. It's empowering.
TULIP:	It's about murder.
PETUNIA:	I thought they were all about murder.
TULIP:	Not all of them. But most are about murder. This particular group explores that thematic element a lot. Dead Ed and the Worthless Sighs.
PETUNIA:	Dead Ed! Yes! Play more Dead Ed!
TULIP:	(*conceding*) Well, if I'm being honest, if you've heard one song, you sorta know their oeuvre. I've had murder on my mind for a while now.
PETUNIA:	Anyone in particular, other than the flowers?
TULIP:	No. Just a constant feeling. . . . It's what I've replaced feeling sorry for myself with.
PETUNIA:	You should come back to the meetings. Maybe we all dream of being murderers.
TULIP:	(*smiling slightly*) I bet Lily dreams of murder. She's got secrets. I can see it in her eyes. The closer we get to losing control, the more our thoughts wander to awful places. Yeah, Lily dreams of killing things.
PETUNIA:	(*looking at the dead flowers*) They never stood a chance, did they?
TULIP:	Better them than the ladies of the Antwerp Gardening Club.
PETUNIA:	True.
TULIP:	I think those closest to us planted these flowers. Though I'm having trouble recalling faces and names.
PETUNIA:	I haven't remembered a face in some time. I can remember the names of flowers though. (*beat*) So who first?

TULIP:	Hmm?
PETUNIA:	Whom should we kill first? Or are tattoos and piercings a good start?
TULIP:	I'm not trying to incite murdering someone.
PETUNIA:	Of course you are! And I think the ladies of the Antwerp Gardening Club are up for it as well. Tattooing be damned. You've convinced me, Tulip. You and Dead Ed.
TULIP:	(*hesitating*) It's just that . . . the drugs. Can I murder the man who gives me the pills?
PETUNIA:	Sure. He's a very nice man, very sweet, but if he must go, then I support your decision. Let's set fire to our living arrangements. Burn it all down! To ashes! Will that work for you? Let's burn down our neighborhood!
TULIP:	(*looking at the dead flowers*) Or . . .
PETUNIA:	Or . . .
TULIP:	I could come to the meeting tomorrow.
PETUNIA:	If you want to, but that seems so small now. Do Dead Ed and the Worthless Sighs have any songs about gardening meetings?

TULIP gives her an absurd glance.

PETUNIA:	Then I seriously doubt a gardening club meeting is going to do it for you. I'll get a knife from my kitchen. A really long one. Rather pointy. Very sharp. Poke, poke! Then we'll see what comes next! This is exciting. Think about what the girls are going to say! This may do wonders for their spirits. The Antwerp Gardening Club needed to kick things up a notch.
TULIP:	I can't tell if you're joking with me.
PETUNIA:	Oh, no. The tattoos were one thing but we are on a completely different level now. This could really boost morale, attendance, you name it. It's the wallowing in the unknown that deals the most damage to the gardening club. Ladies, unite! Let's commit to foul work!
TULIP:	Or . . .

PETUNIA: Or?

TULIP: The meeting might save a few lives.

PETUNIA: Nope. Not sold on that. They're all goners. We're all on a time table. Drugs or no drugs. Lemon meringue spritzer or no lemon meringue spritzer. Tulip, thank you. Finally, a reason to go to this pathetic gathering.

A beat.

TULIP: No. Thank you. The meeting's at what time tomorrow?

PETUNIA: 9 AM sharp. I'll knock on your door.

TULIP: Maybe I'll knock on yours first.

PETUNIA: And I'll bring the knives.

TULIP: Save them. I have one or two of my own. (*starts to exit, then turns*)   You should get a knife tattoo. For battle.

TULIP smiles slightly and exits. PETUNIA does as well.

BLACKOUT. END OF PLAY.

There Are
No Words For This

(all action, no dialogue)

One of the things I like to do with actors and directors is to make them work in silence. Silence is incredibly dramatic. Young actors try to fill every moment with sound, adding the not-so-occasional "um," "oh," or other paralanguage to the scene, even when they have particular lines or, even better, a unique physical choice to fit the situation. They cannot stand silence. They fear it. And even directors forget about or disregard the power of silence, often concentrating so hard to make sure the lines are given the life they deserve that they ignore what's between the lines, underneath them. But playwrights hear their lines as they write. They hear tempo, pitch, and rhythm. Some playwrights may even indicate silence by noting beats or pauses. Silence is precise. Directors need to understand how incredibly focusing it can be for an audience. In silence, the viewer has no choice but to concentrate on the visual, on the physical. And for the actor, silence thins their tightrope. An actor must work with clarity and precision.

In celebration of silence, the following plays are presented here. How about when there are no lines on the page? What then? Directors and actors, have at it! The following short plays do just that. This is not a new exercise. In fact, there may be others like this. The first piece was actually done as an exercise at the suggestion of my dear friend, director and playwright Steve Burch, a long-time theatre professor at the University of Alabama. But here we are! Enjoy the journey!

❧ Adventure ❧

An old man and a boy sit down to play a game of checkers, but what starts simply evolves rapidly into a frenetic and cooperative search-and-rescue mission.

Page-to-Stage Challenges:
- No dialogue
- Very young versus very old characters
- Lots of action—flexible staging

Questions to Ponder/Answers to Seek:
- How does the age of the characters affect the physical choices in the play?
- How can changes in tempo and pace affect the story?
- How do desire, success, and failure affect elements of the play—character relationships, mood, action, and choice?

Adventure

a joust

Characters:

Old Man   Very frail, cane at his side.

Boy   Fresh-faced, eager, smiling.

Setting   A porch. Exterior.

A porch that wraps around an old house. Sitting on the porch is a very frail, old man in a worn-out rocking chair. He is very still, with only an occasional sway of the chair to indicate life.

After a moment, a young Boy enters from the front door. He looks up at the man. The Old Man smiles and nods, which brings a reciprocal smile to the Boy's face and energizes him.

The Boy runs over to an old crate and pulls out a dusty, worn metal container. Opening it, he pulls out a checkerboard, unfolds it, and then dumps out the checkers on the porch. The checkers scatter.

The Old Man rocks back and forth in his chair with slightly more energy. He looks as if he wants to address the Boy, but decides to just observe instead. The Boy looks over at the man for an apology but the man just stares back.

The Boy gathers up the checkers slowly, but his hands are small and many of the checkers fall from his hands and roll around the porch. The Boy doesn't stop. He places the ones he's managed to hold in a pile at the foot of the Old Man and his rocker. The Old Man giggles slightly but he reaches for his cane hanging on the arm of the rocker.

The Old Man begins to direct the Boy with the cane, pointing here and there toward the scattered checkers. The action becomes more and more frenetic, even game-like as the Boy focuses hard on the cane, watches for the Old Man to point in a direction then furiously runs toward the stray checker to gather it up. With each retrieval, the Boy's joy seems to build as does the Old Man's energy. Finally, after several fast retrievals, even the Old Man's cane movements have become more grandiose. The energy in his body, even the rocking motion seem to be stronger as the Boy succeeds again and again in discovering and gathering the checkers. Then there is a pause as the man struggles to locate any remaining checkers. The Boy searches as well, scanning the porch, the edges, even over the porch railing into the yard, hoping for just one more chance to prove himself. The Boy looks back at the Old Man. The Old Man meets the Boy's glance. After a tense, happy moment, the Old Man's cane droops from its outstretched position from the last checker found and touches the ground with a tap. The man lets out a long sigh.

The Boy moves to the pile of checkers and the board. He takes the old crate that the checkers were in, moves it between himself and the Old Man's rocker, and turns it over. He places the checkerboard on the table and begins to set up the checkers, ready for a game.

The Old Man reaches down slightly and touches the Boy's head. Then he takes his cane and "knights" the Boy, tapping the cane on each of his shoulders. The Boy looks up at the Old Man then back at the board. He makes his first move.

BLACKOUT. END OF PLAY.

❧ Ritual ❧

Two religious figures attempt to go through daily contemplations but something unspoken challenges one of them to cease their routine and defy their oaths.

Page-to-Stage Challenges:
- No dialogue
- Clear physical choices
- Focus and connection with scene partner
- Playing with levels and position to create a dynamic visual story

Questions to Ponder/Answers to Seek:
- What troubles each character?
- How do the struggles of each character manifest physically?
- How do the relationships between the two characters change and how does this change affect the mood and tempos of the play?

Ritual

a resistance

Characters:

X   A religious figure.

Y   A religious figure.

Setting   A small chamber for contemplation and reflection.

AT RISE, a religious figure in robes (X) enters, moves to the middle of the room, kneels, and bows their head to pray. After a moment, X shakes their head slightly. Then a beat later, shakes their head more passionately as if trying to win an argument. Another moment passes, then a second religious figure (Y) enters the chamber. X hears Y enter and immediately rises to face Y.

X bends their knees or bows to **Y**.

Y bends their knees or bows to **X**.

X gestures a greeting.

Y returns the welcome.

X makes a religious gesture marking supplication.

Y makes a religious gesture noting gratitude. Then **Y** gestures for **X** to continue their ritual.

X nods and moves to original kneeling position. **X** bows their head, but then looks over their shoulder nervously.

Y moves to **X** and puts a hand on **X**'s shoulder.

X opens their eyes and peers up at **Y**.

Y gestures for **X** to continue.

X shakes their head and removes **Y**'s hand from their shoulder.

Y gestures again with authority.

X rises to face **Y**.

Y slaps X.

X continues to stare defiantly.

Y raises their hand to strike again. X rises to stop Y. X challenges Y.

Y holds out their hand to X.

X begins to turn away from X and begins to move.

Y stops X and turns X back around to face Y. Y stares at X. Then extends a hand, palm up to X.

X stares at Y for a moment.

Y holds firm with their palm extended.

X suddenly slaps Y.

Y holds firm with their palm extended.

X shoves Y. Y stands firm with their palm extended. X shoves Y again. Y falls to the ground.

Y rises, moves back to face X, and extends their palm once again.

X begins to gesture and jerk erratically about the chamber without words, on the verge of speaking.

Y watches earnestly. Y then also joins X in the erratic "dance."

X sees Y join them and suddenly stops, watching Y move about.

Y's fit slowly fades.

X begins to smile. Y stares at X, then smiles.

X moves to their initial spot, kneels and bows their head.

Y stares on at X over their shoulder.

BLACKOUT. END OF PLAY.